The LOST E
(Shoulda..)
    (Coulda...)
                (Woulda....been)

Curb Your Enthusiasm

By Ray DiSilvestro &
John Miller

Copyright © Ray DiSilvestro - John Miller, 2013

All rights reserved. This book or any portion thereof
may not be reproduced or used in any manner whatsoever
without the express written permission of the publisher
except for the use of brief quotations in a book review.

Printed in the United States of America

First Printing, 2013

ISBN-13:978-1491081624

Inquiries and comments: Bigcarlproductions@gmail.com

Note: All characters appearing in this work are fictitious. Any resemblance to real persons (living or dead, or useless), places and incidents is purely coincidental. No animals or celebrities were used in trial tests of this material.

Dedicated to the cast and crew of Curb Your Enthusiasm, with special acknowledgement to Larry David and Jeff Garlin, for their inspiration, encouragement and guidance.

Table of Contents

Read Me First vii
The DEFINING moment (*the Definition*) ix
1. GENESIS – In the Beginning… 1
2. Episode 1 – **My SPACE** 4
3. Writing – Snippets to Scenes 20
4. Episode 2 – ***Ms.* Potatohead** 22
5. Creativity – Trading the Ponies 39
6. Episode 3 – **The Princess and the PEE** 42
7. Editing – Tense and Tension 56
8. Episode 4 – **Good Things Come to Those Who Weigh(t)** 58
9. Where ARE You? *Standing Around…* 77
10. Episode 5 – **Cluck YOU!** 79
11. Reaching Out – First Contact 96
12. Episode 6 – **Time Heals NO Wounds** 98
13. Inspiration - Treasures from Trash 116
14. Episode 7 – **The Gifts That Keep on Giving** 119
15. Striking Out - Stalking the BIG SHOTS 134
16. Episode 8 – **Hairs Looking at You, Kid** 136
17. Ironies – Up Close *and* Personal 150
18. Episode 9 – **Scriptably Soft** 152
19. Mis-Perception and Miss Confection 164
20. Episode 10 – **HOT, Crossed, Buns** 167
21. BUT WAIT! THERE'S MORE! VOLUME 2 181

[v]

READ ME FIRST. Trust us, it gets better....

This page is boring...but trust us, it gets better, MUCH better. This book is written in a style that alternates insights and narrative of its development with script-like outline-episodes of a sitcom. The sitcom we wrote mimics the style of the HBO comedy series, Curb Your Enthusiasm. These 'Lost' episodes are not so much 'Lost', but more accurately, 'Never Found'. Our original intention was to put together a few samples of our creative abilities to showcase our talent. Creating the material was EASY. Placing the finished work with anyone who might get it produced was anything but EASY.

We started out writing a generic sitcom episode. As it grew into multiple episodes, we found that generic character names were difficult to follow and identify with. Ultimately, as a tribute to one of the people that inspired our writing, the material we created follows a format similar to that used in the production and filming of Curb Your Enthusiasm. The scenes are labeled with minimal scene setup identified. Concepts and ideas are introduced, and in some cases exact character dialog/lines are supplied. In others, room for 'improv' on the part of any given character is denoted, similar to the improv-comedy utilized in the production of Curb Your Enthusiasm.

Each episode outline begins with a cover page identifying the episode title, a short synopsis of the episode and the cast, including special guests. Each outline scene leads off with an identifier. For example:

3. EXT. LARRY IN HIS CAR, DRIVING INTO DOCTORS OFFICE BUILDING PARKING LOT – DAY (ONE)

This denotes Scene #3 is an exterior (EXT) scene, on day number one of the episode. The named character (Larry) is driving in his car and the setting for the scene is the parking lot of an office building. The scene to scene transitions rely on the ability of the reader (viewer) to grasp and visualize the change in settings. For example, if a scene ends with the characters leaving an interior (INT) setting and the next scene is an exterior (EXT) shot, it's presumed that the characters walked outside. We chose not to include explicit scene transition notes unless there was a particularly complex scene change. Unless otherwise noted, scenes end with a 'fade out to black' and begin with a 'fade in from black'.

Each episode has a theme or 'hook' which is the main thrust of the episode while one or more subplots are inserted to add some comic diversions. In addition to each episode 'hook', there is a distinct-recurring theme that is referenced in every episode in this volume as well as the next. Look to the next page and discover the distinct, **DEFINING** theme.

DEFINITION:

***DEGNER*:** noun, verb, Degner·ing, interjection <u>Vulgar</u>.

noun
1. excrement; feces.
2. an act of defecating; evacuation: Pull over, I have to take a *degner*;
3. the degners, diarrhea.
4. Slang. pretense, lies, exaggeration, or nonsense.
5. Slang. something inferior or worthless.

verb (used with object)
6. Slang. to exaggerate or lie to.
7. Slang. to defecate in (one's clothes), as from terror or illness; soil (oneself): She was so shocked, she *degnered* her pants!

GENESIS – In the Beginning........

In the beginning...there was darkness. We (Ray and John) weren't creating a new world. We weren't writing sitcom scripts. We definitely weren't writing a book. We weren't even writers (by trade). We were in the technology field, responsible for a major upgrade to one of our company locations. We had our choice of one of five corporate locations: Chicago, Denver, Washington, D.C., San Francisco, and Los Angeles. By 'choice of locations', that really meant only San Francisco or Los Angeles. We were based out of Chicago and our Manager, a.k.a. the World's WORST Boss had already let his 'preferred' staff choose before us. No one wanted to commute Monday thru Friday to LA or San Francisco for the next 18 months. After thorough analysis of the variables and careful consideration of circumstances, we chose LA...because it was winter in Chicago.

The work was terrible. It was night shift work starting around midnight and lasting until 5 in the morning. Combined with a 2000 mile flight twice a week, we wore out quickly. The DOPE that masqueraded as our manager poured gas on the fire with encouraging emails such as: *"A good plan violently executed today is better than a perfect plan executed tomorrow"*, and our personal favorite: *"Losers whine about doing their best, winners go home and fuck the prom queen."* And so began our MOTIVATION.

By chance, those endless cross country flights offered episodes of the HBO comedy series, Curb Your Enthusiasm on the inflight video. We were both admirers of the show and would occasionally remark to one another how surreal our own lives and experiences were. We continued to joke that *WE* could write material as funny, or even funnier than the Curb episodes we had just seen.

[1]

Working nights in LA meant having days OFF, which in turn led to sitting at sidewalk cafes and telling insanely funny real-life stories until we were spitting coffee. Regularly, one of us would say, "We should be writing this stuff down--it's GOLD." Waiters and waitresses that heard our 'material' wanted to know if we were writers developing TV content. When we would tell them we weren't, we were just relating true stories, they all said the same thing: "You guys should be writing this stuff down." So we did.

Over the next year, the World's WORST Boss inspired us so often and to such levels that a few stories quickly evolved to nearly three seasons of sitcom episodes. With the obvious parallels to Curb Your Enthusiasm, we began to tailor and tune our work into script-outlines that followed the Curb format. We began researching Curb Your Enthusiasm. We absorbed every news story, every cast or crew member interview, every piece of material related to Curb and the production of the series. With rumors that Season 8 would be the last for an indefinite period of time, we figured handing two seasons (20 episodes) of turn-key material to someone like Larry David would be a slam dunk.

We weren't (and still aren't) in it for the money. A writing credit and maybe some expense money, and we could turn this stuff out until the end of time. What could be easier? One of the teaser phrases we would throw at each other, and still do is: "ENVISION IT." Of course we overlooked a few key details while 'envisioning' IT, but we weren't smart enough to know that it might derail us. So we pressed on, motivation undeterred. We continued to generate ideas and material that filled the backs of menus, cocktail napkins, and anything else we could scribble on.

To summarize from Genesis: The World's WORST Boss created a world (a project in LA) for us and appointed us as his regent*. We proved disobedient and the World's WORST Boss tried to destroy us and our world (project) with his presumed POWER: flood(ing) us with threatening email and text messages. And...that's about all the biblical crossover there was. We weren't destroyed. Each and every success on our part only served to further infuriate the World's WORST Boss, which further motivated us and provided even more creative material. The World's WORST Boss' final maneuver was childish and parental. In an attempt to intimidate us, he would get 'in our face' and violate our personal space, which gave us the foundation for......

* - *Jesus wouldn't like that we stole this (and corrupted it) from his dad's book. Sorry, man.*

Episode 1

"My SPACE"

Synopsis: Larry's personal space is repeatedly violated by mannerless jerks until fate hands Larry the ultimate 'weapon' to even the score.

Scenes: 19

Cast: Larry, Jeff, Unnamed woman driver, Doctor, HBO office worker, restaurant staff, clothing store clerks.

Special Guest: Tim Curry or Milo O'Shea as the Elevator Operator.

"My SPACE"

1. INT. PUBLIC BATHROOM – DAY (ONE)

Larry is in a completely empty public bathroom (*layout is 2 urinals on one wall and 4 on the opposite wall*). Larry looks around and hesitantly approaches the wall with 2 urinals and starts to unzip his pants. Immediately, (*from off camera*) an unnamed person appears and takes the urinal next to Larry.

Larry (to person): "REALLY? You're going to use THAT one?"

The unnamed person ignores Larry. The unnamed person answers his ringing cell phone (Bluetooth earpiece), and begins to gesture while talking, moving his hands from the urinal into Larry's 'space'.

Larry (to person): "REALLY????"

The unnamed person starts to turn his body towards Larry, ignoring Larry's presence. Larry jumps back.

Larry: "Ok, we're DONE here." (*awkwardly walking away and zipping up at the same time.*)

2. EXT. LARRY IN HIS CAR - DAY (ONE)

Larry is driving in his car, placing a call to Jeff (Jeff answers-unheard). At a stoplight, a charity donation collector stands at/leans in the open window of Larry's car with a donation box. Larry waves him off but the collector does not leave. Larry is speaking on his cellphone to Jeff, confirming their lunch meeting for the next day.

Larry (to collector): "Sorry, I only have 100's."

Larry starts to drive off forcing the collector to jump back from the moving car. Larry tells Jeff he has to hang up because he's on his way to his doctor's office. Larry tells Jeff they can catch up when they meet for lunch and ends the call.

3. EXT. LARRY IN HIS CAR DRIVING INTO DOCTORS OFFICE BUILDING PARKING LOT – DAY (ONE)

Larry and an unnamed woman driver approach the same single open parking spot from different directions. Larry is slightly closer and switches on his turn signal. The woman driver speeds up and makes a sharp turn into the spot and 'steals' it. Larry parks in the next row and confronts the woman driver after he exits his car.

Larry: "That was MY Space. I was there first. I signaled for God's sake...I was already turning."

Woman driver: "It's a PUBLIC space. There's no sign that says 'RESERVED for bald headed WINDBAGS', is there? Do you see a sign?"

Larry: "But I was there first. It was MY space."

Woman driver (walking away): "Yeah……blow it out your ass, WINDBAG."

Larry (yelling after her): "IT was MY Space..."

4. INT. DOCTOR'S OFFICE BUILDING LOBBY, AT ELEVATOR – DAY (ONE)

The Elevator door opens and Larry enters the elevator. The elevator is staffed by an operator. The operator is an older, 'crusty' type, with a heavy Irish accent and has an oversized/prominent nametag that reads: Doyle DEGNER. Larry reaches for the floor button at same time as the operator. The operator tells Larry he's the only one that can operate the elevator. Larry makes a crack a about career path and job training. The elevator operator gives Larry a dirty look/scowl.

Elevator Operator (barks out): "Floor?"

Larry (replies): "Twenty-two."

Elevator Operator (repeats): "Twenty TOOT."

Larry: "Toot???"

Elevator Operator: "Yessir, Twenty TOOT."

The elevator operator presses button 22, the doors close and the car lurches. While going up, the operator unbuttons/unzips and drops his pants to tuck in his shirt. Larry is offended.

Larry (to operator): "I'm standing RIGHT HERE...I can SEE you."

Elevator Operator (responds defiantly): "Well now, it's not your private space is it?? I mean, there's no 'wee' sign, is there?"

Larry (argues): "It IS PRIVATE. I don't need to see your underwear...or anything else."

The elevator arrives and the doors open.
Elevator Operator (to Larry): "Yeah????...blow it out yur arse, ya WINDBAG."

Larry exits, looking back in disbelief.

Larry (yells as the elevator door closes): "PRIVATE. It IS a private space...schmohawk."

5. INT. DOCTOR'S OFFICE EXAMINING ROOM – DAY (ONE)

A doctor is reviewing Larry's chart in the examining room and speaking to Larry. The doctor suggests a specific antibiotic medication as treatment for Larry's condition, and warns of possible side effects.

Larry: "Side effects? WHAT? My hair's going to fall out??"

Doctor (getting too close to Larry's face): "Larry, it may trigger minor gastritis...you know, indigestion. Here...take these samples and I'll get a regular prescription written."

The doctor hands Larry sample packets of the medications and leaves the room to write the prescription. Larry opens the sample pack (two tablets), uses the in-room sink to fill a paper cup and swallows both tablets. The doctor returns and reads the prescription to Larry.

Doctor: "Fill this today and take ONE tablet with a meal."

Larry: "One?...with a meal???"

Doctor: "Yes, ONE, with any meal or any snack–it will minimize the gas."

Larry leaves the Doctor's office, pressing on his stomach in discomfort.

[SCENE TRANSITION]

6. INT. AT ELEVATOR OUTSIDE DOCTOR'S OFFICE – DAY (ONE)

Larry is waiting for the elevator, occasionally rubbing his stomach. The elevator arrives after a lengthy wait (Larry is repeatedly pressing the call button). Larry passes a 'squeaker' fart, quickly looks left and right, and 'fans' the seat of his pants. The elevator doors open slowly. The operator recognizes Larry.

Elevator Operator: "Ahh, welcome back, Mr. Privacy."

Larry (irritated by the lengthy wait): "What...did you LOSE the directions to 22?"

Larry has gas pressure (*clutches his stomach and pulls at the waistband of his pants*). Larry farts (silently) on the way down to the ground floor (*makes slight convulsion movement and 'fans' the seat of his pants*).

Elevator Operator (snippy, in a heavy Irish accent): "What da hell... did you just airbrush 'yur' boxers? (*fanning his hand under his nose*)"

The elevator doors open. Larry pauses, stares at his oversized nametag (Doyle DEGNER), and exits the elevator.

7. EXT. DOCTORS OFFICE BUILDING PARKING LOT – DAY (ONE)

Larry is walking to his car and notices a clothing store across the parking lot. Larry changes direction and walks towards the clothing store.

[SCENE TRANSITION]

8. INT. CLOTHING STORE - DAY (ONE)

Larry is inside the clothing store and has selected a pair of pants. He is shown to a fitting room by a clerk and enters the fitting room. Larry closes the door and turns the 'button' lock on the door knob. Larry has removed his pants and is starting to pull on the new pants when the fitting room door knob rattles.

Larry: "OCCUPIED."

The fitting room clerk forces the door open and bursts into the changing room, face to face with Larry.

Larry: "IM IN HERE."

Clerk: "Yes, you ARE...do you require any assistance?"

Larry: "Yes...I require that you GET OUT of here."

The clerk leaves. Larry removes the new pants while holding one hand against the door, and struggles to put his own pants back on. Larry storms out of the store, (visibly irritated).

9. INT. RESTAURANT - DAY (TWO)

Larry enters the restaurant and approaches the hostess.

Larry: "Greene, party of 2."

Hostess: "Yes, let me check."

The hostess looks down at the reservations book and does not look back up (as if asleep). Larry, waiting for the hostess to look up, asks the bartender for glass of water and takes a prescription pill. The hostess looks up (as if jarred awake) and takes Larry to Jeff's table. Seated at the table, Larry tells Jeff about his run-in with the elevator operator who dropped his pants while the two of them were in the elevator and how later, the clothing store clerk got into his 'personal space'. Larry tells Jeff about taking the two prescription pills without eating and how it gave him terrible gas. Larry says he thought he 'shart' his pants while riding down the elevator.

Jeff: "Shart? –what is SHART?"

Larry (explains to Jeff): "You know, shart. It's like a fart, only you accidentally shit with the fart…a shit-fart…SHART."

Jeff (acknowledges): "Ahhh, shart. Yep…been there. I've bought several new pairs of underwear that way."

They continue to chat. Larry tells Jeff they need to order.

Larry: "Let's order. I already took the pill and I'm supposed to take it with a meal."

Jeff: "That's not what 'take with a meal' means. It means you're supposed to take it AFTER you have food in your stomach."

Larry: "Really?.....eiiiyyy."
Larry feels gas pressure begin to build and grimaces while rubbing his stomach. Larry tells Jeff he needs to use the restroom and stands up (*rubbing his stomach as he tugs at the waistband of his pants*).

[SCENE TRANSITION]

10. INT. RESTAURANT BATHROOM AREA - DAY (TWO)
Larry approaches the restroom. It is a unisex type (men or women). Larry looks in, enters and closes the door. The sliding lock is flimsy. Larry double checks the door to see that it doesn't open, turns, lowers his pants, and checks the underwear for SHART marks. Larry sits on the toilet. The door knob rattles. Larry snaps/turns his head to look at door lock and reaches up with his hand to brace the door (just out of reach).

Larry (shouting): "I'm IN HERE."

The person standing on the other side of the door, turning the handle, is the rude woman driver from the doctor's office parking lot. (*Audio dub: toilet flush noise*). The door opens and Larry exits the bathroom.

Woman (to Larry): "Oh, Mr. MY SPACE."

Larry (to woman): "Yes…and this is a public space. Enjoy."

The rude woman enters the bathroom and closes the door. Larry walks away smirking. The rude woman (*audible only, from behind the closed door*): 'Jesus Christ, did something die in here?'

[*SCENE TRANSITION*]

11. INT. RESTAURANT - DAY (TWO)
Larry returns to the table (smiling).

Jeff (to Larry): "What's going on?"

Larry: "Nothing. Someone just needed some 'SPACE', and I gave it to her."

Jeff: "Ok...want to get in a round of golf tomorrow morning?"

Larry: "Can't. I have that thing over at HBO."

12. INT. HBO OFFICE CONFERENCE ROOM – DAY (THREE)
Larry is sitting in a conference room by himself making a phone call to his doctor. Larry attempts to get through directly to the doctor but is forced to speak to the doctor's 'triage' nurse. Larry tells her about the terrible gas/farting caused by the prescribed medications and that he needs relief. In the mist of the conversation, an unnamed HBO office-worker opens the conference room door and stands in the doorway. Larry waves her off/points to the phone. The office worker nods 'yes' to Larry in acknowledgement. Larry looks back at his appointment book and asks (into the phone) if it's possible to see the doctor today. Larry looks back up and notices the office worker is still in the doorway.

Larry (irritated, covering the phone, looking at the office worker): "I'm IN HERE."

The office worker nods ('yes') in acknowledgement to Larry but does not close the door or back out.

Larry (to the office worker, covering the phone): "I'll be done in one minute."

The office worker nods ('yes') to Larry and proceeds to walk all the way in to the room and sits down.

Larry (into phone): "I'll be right over."
Larry abruptly hangs up the phone.

Larry (passing the office worker seated at the table, pauses): "REALLY? You just come in and sit down?"

The office worker is oblivious.

13. EXT. DOCTOR'S OFFICE BUILDING PARKING LOT – DAY (THREE)

Larry is in his car returning to the doctor's office, driving through the parking lot. The unnamed rude woman driver from the previous day is backing out of a parking spot in front of Larry. Larry approaches in his car and signals. The rude woman driver sees Larry waiting/signaling for the spot and backs out of her spot blocking Larry. The rude woman driver pauses briefly as another car approaches from the other direction and takes the empty space.

Larry (yelling at her as she drives away): "THAT WAS MY SPACE…MINE."

The woman driver mouths 'WINDBAG' as she drives past.

14. INT. DOCTOR'S OFFICE BUILDING LOBBY - DAY (THREE)

Larry approaches the elevator. The elevator door is open but no one is inside. A sign is taped in front of /covering the buttons. Larry reads the sign out loud (*camera close-up of sign*).

Larry: "Be RIGHT Back–Taking a five.DEGNER."

Larry repeats: "Taking...a...Degner?"

Larry tosses the sign aside and presses 22. The doors close and Larry proceeds up to 22.

15. INT. DOCTOR'S OFFICE EXAMINING ROOM – DAY (THREE)

Larry is with the doctor discussing the gas distress from the medication prescribed. The doctor suggests an additional medication. He describes it as an anti-gas drug.

Doctor (getting too close to Larry's face--Larry backs up): "Larry, it may have some minor side effects."

Larry: "Come on Doc, I'm practically splitting apart at the stomach. What kind of side-effects?"

Doctor: "It may cause some minor cramping. Here, take these samples and I'll get a regular prescription written."

The doctor hands Larry a sample packet of the medications and leaves the room to get the prescription. Larry opens the sample pack (two tablets) and uses the in-room sink to fill a paper cup and swallows one tablet. The doctor returns and reads the prescription notes to Larry.

Doctor: "Fill this and take ONE tablet whenever you take the other medication."

Larry: "One, got it...with the OTHER medication?"

Doctor: "Yes–only when you take the other prescription – don't take it by itself, it'll rip through you like a tornado through a trailer park."

Larry leaves the doctor's office, rubbing his stomach in discomfort.

[*SCENE TRANSITION*]

16. INT. AT ELEVATOR OUTSIDE DOCTOR'S OFFICE – DAY (THREE)

Larry presses the elevator call button. The elevator arrives after a lengthy wait and slowly opens. The operator recognizes Larry and is visibly aggravated.

Elevator Operator (to Larry in heavy Irish accent): "Will we be needin' an air freshener or a shovel today, Governor Windbag?"

Larry: (rubbing his stomach and grimacing): "First floor."

Elevator Operator (holding the door open extra long): "We'll be needin' all the fresh air we can get now, won't we?"

Larry (repeats, slightly urgent tone):"ONE, please."

The Operator presses 10.

Larry (contorts face): "I said, ONE. ONE!"

Larry continues to clutch his stomach (*does a small convulse*). The elevator operator presses 11.

Elevator Operator: "Dare ya go, one-one."

The elevator Operator makes a BIG production of each floor arrival (announcing each floor and looking down the hall). As the elevator approaches the ground floor, Larry loudly/longly farts (*audio dub*).

Elevator Operator: "Whad now? You fouled me car."

Larry (to Operator): "It's not your private space is it? I mean, there's no sign, is there?"

Elevator Operator (fanning under his nose): "For Godssake, whad er ya doin'?"

Larry stares at the operator's nametag and then at the 'Taking a five.Degner' sign.

Larry (replies as the elevator door opens): "I'm taking ….a DEGNER."

Larry exits the elevator, makes a slight convulsion movement and tugs at the seat of his pants.

Larry: "ahhhhgggh…"

17. EXT. DOCTORS OFFICE BUILDING PARKING LOT – DAY (THREE)

Larry looks around the parking lot and notices the clothing

store (from the previous visit) across the parking lot. Larry walks awkwardly towards it, tugging at the seat of his pants as he walks/limps.

18. INT. CLOTHING STORE - DAY (THREE)

Larry, carrying a package of underwear and new pants, is shown to and enters a fitting room. Larry closes the door and turns the 'button' lock on the door knob. Larry is opening the package when the fitting room door knob 'rattles'.

Larry: "I'm IN HERE."

Larry grabs the door handle and braces the door.

Fitting room clerk: "Yes, you ARE... Do you require any assistance?"

The clerk continues turning the handle but cannot get in.

Larry: "Yes, I require you get AWAY from here."

The clerk leaves. Larry makes a slight convulsion movement, tugs at the seat of his pants, looks at the new pants and nods his head ('no'). Larry takes the new pants and underwear to the register and 'expedites' the purchase (*throws cash the on counter*). Larry's stomach rumbles (*audio dub*) and Larry clutches it and grimaces. Larry asks the checkout clerk for directions to the bathroom and is directed to it.

[*SCENE TRANSITION*]

19. INT. CLOTHING STORE BATHROOM - DAY (THREE)

Larry enters the clothing store restroom and approaches one of two stalls (the other is occupied). Larry places the new pants on a shelf and sits down on the toilet. Larry looks for the toilet paper roller on both side walls. Nothing is found. Larry twists around to see that the roller is above and behind the toilet. Larry is forced to stand to reach the roller. The toilet paper roll only dispenses/tears 1 sheet at a time. Larry yanks at the roll in frustration. The roll pops out and falls into the toilet. Larry looks under the stall wall, sees the adjoining stall is occupied, and knocks on the divider (no reply). Larry asks (under the divider) for toilet paper (no reply). Larry stands on the toilet, looks over the divider and asks the person in the adjoining stall for toilet paper. (The person in the stall is the fitting room clerk from the previous scene).

Fitting room clerk (looks up and yells - horrified): "I'm IN HERE."

Larry: "Yes, you ARE…and NOW I require some assistance."

FADE OUT/Cue Music.

(END)

- 3 -

WRITING – Snippets to Scenes

After testing out a story on...well, anyone that would listen, someone would occasionally ask, "where do you get your ideas from?" And it would be Hollywood–correct to say, "We stole it ALL." But that would be a lie (which is also, ironically, a Hollywood trait). In fact, our story ideas were incredibly easy to come by. To say that the two of us had led interesting lives (prior to meeting at our jobs) would be an understatement. Most of the storylines are based on personal, true events. Some are based on stories we read in newspapers or saw on TV. And some are a combination of both – taking the truly bizarre stories that pass for 'news' and mixing in some flavor from our pasts and current on-the-job experiences.

Capturing the material was never too difficult. We would routinely send text messages to each other when an idea or storyline came to one of us and the other would help fill in details during the back-and-forth messages. Other times, it meant writing story ideas on everything from cocktail napkins to the backs of paystubs. We had a simple 2-line test for the material we were creating:

      1). Is it outrageous?

      2). Is it offensive?

It would generally follow that it was FUNNY if it met the 2-line test. Eventually, we had a folder with thousands of notes and ideas. Occasionally, we even repeated ourselves, not realizing that we had created nearly identical material many months earlier. The time came to compile our material, so we lazily typed it into a spreadsheet and organized it.

We were shocked. The list quickly ran up to 2000 entries --- everything from 1-scene filler ideas to complete storyline-episode ideas. It grew by the week. Once we realized we were literally throwing away good material because we failed to write it down, we made a point to record everything, no matter how (scribbled on a napkin) or where (the middle of a funeral). The list jumped to 2500 entries within a few weeks...and still we hadn't written any full episode-outlines.

We had a loose collection of parts that needed to be assembled into a finished product. Clearly, not all the parts would fit together properly. After some trial-and-error, and a few trips to the parts-bin (idea spreadsheet), we had a fully baked...............

Episode 2

"*Ms.* POTATOHEAD"

Synopsis: Larry dates a woman whose philosophy AND physical appearance aren't what they seem and eventually finds himself confounded by an evening of 'loose' parts. Meanwhile, Larry's buxom office temp leaves a string of jealousy in her wake as she bounces between Larry's friends, until the federal authorities become involved.

Scenes: 14

Cast: Larry, Jeff, Susie, Leon, Richard; HOT Office Temp (Insa), Larry's Girlfriend (Cabeca), Richard's Girlfriend (Los), Un-named police officer, Un-named old lady, misc. restaurant staff.

Special Guest: Un-named INS agent – Erik Estrada.

"*Ms.* POTATOHEAD"

1. INT. LARRY'S HOUSE - DAY (ONE)
Larry is sitting on the floor of his living room – a box of parts in front of him and an instruction sheet in his hands.

Larry (*reading out loud*): "Thank you purchase Executive Massage chair. We hope it bring you many year of happy moment endings. Assembly is you required. You are Tool required: Ratchet Torque Wrench..."

Larry: "Can you believe this crap,(*pause*) I'm a TOOL??? And what the HELL is a Ratchet Torque Wrench??? (*pause*) LEON?"

Leon explains the wrench and asks Larry where he keeps his tools.

Larry: "I don't own any tools."

Leon: "No Tools? Damn. Every REAL man has tools, Larry. You gots to have tools if you're gonna be THE Man."

Larry says he will go out and buy tools immediately.

2. EXT. LARRY'S CAR - DAY (ONE)
Larry is driving his car on a city street. Larry's car horn has an electrical short and intermittently sounds as he's driving. Larry repeatedly taps on the steering wheel after it spontaneously honks in an effort to make it stop. Larry pulls up to the intersection. An elderly woman is crossing the street and the horn sounds. The elderly woman, without hesitation or looking up, bangs the hood of Larry's car with her purse. Larry apologizes/explains (out the

window) about the faulty horn. The elderly woman gives Larry the finger. Larry drives up the street. Larry encounters a car blocking both lanes, trying to turn left from the right lane. Larry tries to use the horn and nothing happens. Larry drives another block, stopping behind a police car at a red-light. The car horn sounds intermittently. The police officer gets out of his car to investigate. Larry explains and proves the horn noise is not intentional by keeping his hands out the window as the horn sounds. The officer tells Larry to go to a nearby auto-parts store and get a replacement or risk a ticket.

3. INT. AUTO PARTS STORE - DAY (ONE)
Larry is waiting in line to get the replacement car part. Larry approaches the woman working the parts counter and they begin to flirt. Larry compliments her earrings and she tells him they aren't 'real'--they are 'bolt-ons'. Larry and the parts-woman continue to banter. Larry makes a 'blow my horn joke'. Larry introduces himself. The parts counter woman introduces herself:

Parts-woman: "I'm Cabeca DeBatata...pleased to meet you."

Larry comments on her exotic name and asks her where it comes from.

Parts-woman /Cabeca: "All around……different parts."

Larry asks her to dinner that evening. The parts-woman/Cabeca agrees.

4. INT. RESTAURANT – DAY/NIGHT (ONE)
Larry and Cabeca are chatting-laughing about Larry's faulty

car horn as they finish dinner. An attractive (tall, thin, large breasted –'Hot') young woman walks up, stops, and says hello to Larry (the woman has a European accent). Larry, (*blatantly staring at her breasts*) introduces the Hot woman to his date as his new office (temp) help.

Larry (to Cabeca): "Cabeca, this is Insa. She's from Romania."

Cabeca displays a smirk.

Larry introduces the Hot Temp to Cabeca.

Larry (to Hot Temp/Insa): "Insa, this is Cabeca...Cabeca DeBatata."

Insa/Hot Temp displays a smirk, says 'good night/see you tomorrow' and walks away. Cabeca makes a remark to Larry about the office temp's 'non OEM' parts and the shameless flirting. Larry disputes the flirting asks her to explain 'non OEM'.

Cabeca: "Non-OEM –you know, not Original Equipment Manufacture...O-E-M(*pause*), she didn't come out that way originally... she has outrageous bolt-ons..."

Larry: "Bolt-ons?"

Cabeca: "Bolt-ons, Larry. Aftermarket accessories...Larry, she has outrageous implants...and uses them as a calling card to flirt with."

Larry agrees but claims not to have noticed. The dinner bill arrives. Larry examines the bill and notices that Cabeca never ordered an entrée, just a collection of appetizers.

Larry (to Cabeca):"Didn't you want an entrée? You're not on one of those crazy diets, are you?"

Cabeca: "Sometimes, the sum of the parts is greater than the WHOLE, Larry."

Larry is puzzled by the remark, disputes it briefly with her, gives her the 'LIE stare', but has difficulty making eye-contact. Larry accepts her reply with an 'OK.'

5. EXT. STREET/PARKING - DAY/NIGHT (ONE)
Larry and Cabeca are parked in front of Cabeca's apartment (end of date). Larry and Cabeca are kissing (enthusiastically). As Larry is kissing her, he runs his fingers through her long hair. Her hair becomes entangled in Larry's fingers and as he pulls his hand back, the hair from Cabeca pulls away from her head and stays in Larry's hand. Larry reacts 'stunned'. Cabeca laughs it off. She tells Larry she always wears a wig whenever she leaves her house.

Cabeca: "It's a low maintenance part."

Larry, still uneasy, agrees about low maintenance (*rubbing his own head*). Cabeca thanks Larry for a great evening as she retrieves her hair out of Larry's hand. Larry thanks her -- trying but (again) failing to make eye-contact (*head bobbing*), suggests they get together later in the week and she agrees. Larry drives away.

6. INT. LARRY'S OFFICE - DAY (TWO)
Larry is talking on a speaker-phone to Cabeca. Larry

thanks her for a great evening the night before and finalizes plans for a dinner date later in the week.

Cabeca (*audio dub*): "Is the fake jugs flirt still working there?"

Larry grabs the phone handset from the phone and switches off the speaker.

Larry: "Jugs?"

Cabeca (*audio dub*): "Come on, Larry (*pause*), Insa is the Romanian word for JUGS."

Larry (staring at Insa/Hot Temp's breasts) tells Cabeca that the temp assignment is up and Insa will be leaving by the end of tomorrow and ends the call. Larry dials Jeff on the phone while staring/nodding reluctantly as he looks across his office at Insa's breasts. Larry tells Jeff he has to (temporarily) get rid of the hot temp Insa---she's causing him problems with his girlfriend Cabeca the parts-woman, and he can't keep her around for now. Jeff offers to take her.

Larry: "It's only temporary...just until I get Cabeca...sorted out."

Larry ends the call and tells Insa (while staring at her breasts) that she is to report to Jeff, just for a few days, starting the next day.

7. INT. LARRY'S HOUSE - DAY (THREE)
Larry is talking to Leon about his next date with Cabeca and is concerned.

Larry (to Leon): "She seems to have a (*pause*) a lazy (*pause*)..."

Leon: "A Lazy WHAT? A Lazy ASS?....Lemmee tell you somthin about lazy bitches..."

Larry: "No, (*pause*) a Lazy...eye. It's distracting. I try and look her in the eye to read her, and it's like a ping-pong game going on up there. And...she wears a wig. She has a (*pause*) crew cut hairstyle (*pause*) maybe it's a militant thing?"

Leon: "Fuck that shit, LD. I like the short hair (rubbing his head)...even if she's bald. It's LOW MAINTENTANCE."

Larry: "Yeah (*pause*), low maintenance (*pause*), she said that."

Leon: "And Fuck it, you're a FREE AGENT, Larry. You need to Hit IT and Quit IT, Understand? HIT IT AND QUIT IT..."

Larry: "Yeah (*pause*), OK."

8. INT. JEFF'S OFFICE - DAY (FOUR)
Jeff is in his office, talking on phone to Larry, thanking him for the hot temp Insa, while looking across office at her breasts. Susie enters the office unannounced. She demands (to Jeff) to know who the hot temp is. Susie berates the hot temp for dressing like a highschool tramp. Jeff abruptly ends his call to Larry.

Susie (to Jeff): "WHO the FUCK is this LITTLE TRAMP? Are you paying for all of her or just THOSE (*gesturing towards Insa's large breasts*)?"

Jeff (explaining to Susie): "It's only temporary (*pause*), Insa is Larry's temp and this is short term."

Susie (to Jeff): "The tramp's name is JUGS?"

Jeff: "What? Jugs? No, her name is Insa..."

Susie: "Did Larry tell you that? Is that SICK fuck playing a joke on you? Are you a moron? Insa is Romanian for JUGS."

Susie tells Jeff off and threatens repercussions if Jeff doesn't get rid of the temp immediately.

Susie: "The only fucking thing around here that's short term will be your life if that TRAMP is still here tomorrow."

Jeff reluctantly agrees.

Jeff: "Yeah, Yeah...get rid of Jugs...Insa by tomorrow."

9. INT. RESTAURANT - DAY (FOUR)

Jeff is seated at a restaurant table. Larry arrives and apologizes for keeping Jeff waiting.

Larry (to Jeff): "Sorry I'm late. I had to use the restroom, (*pause*). Someone left a major degner in there and I had to wait for it to air out."

Larry sits and asks Jeff how the hot temp, Insa is working out.

Jeff: "I have to get rid of her by tomorrow or Susie will cut my balls off, put them in a blender and feed them to me as a breakfast smoothie." (*pauses/sighs/shakes head.*)

Larry: "What happened?"

Jeff: "Did you know 'Insa' was Romanian for 'Jugs'?"

Larry: "How did you (*pause*), yes (*pause*), my girlfriend Cabeca told me that just the other day."

Jeff: "Yeah, Susie told me right after she saw Insa at my office (*pause*). Your girlfriend's name is Rebecca?"

Larry: "No. It's Cabeca. Cabeca DeBatata. PRETTY exotic, right?"

Jeff (laughing): "Well, sort of..."

Larry: "What's so funny?"

Jeff: "Larry(*pause*), uhhhhm, Cabeca DeBatata (*laughing*), it's Portuguese for potato head."

Larry: "What are you, the Rosetta Stone? More like the Rosetta boulder. You know what? Jeff is Portuguese for BULLSHIT."

Larry tells Jeff he can't take the hot temp/Insa back right now because Cabeca has a real bug up her tuchus about her. Larry suggests finding another spot for her.

Jeff: "Yeah—someone harmless. Someone that could keep her temporarily."

Richard Lewis enters the scene and greets Larry and Jeff.

Richard: "I can't join you, I'm having lunch with my girlfriend, Los. (*Richard points her out at another table in the restaurant*)"

Larry asks Richard about his girlfriend.

Larry: "Is the relationship going along ok (*pause*), it's solid, right?"

Richard: "It's good...WHY? What have you heard? Never mind (*pause*) Los is a little neurotic, and a bit of a neat freak...but WHO am I to throw stones, right?"

Larry (repeats out loud): "A bit of a neat freak."

Larry nudges Jeff and nods towards Richard.

Jeff: "Richard (*pause*), maybe I can help you out..."

Jeff explains that he has a very skilled office temp that Susie doesn't like and he needs to place her somewhere temporarily. Richard declines and says his girlfriend is the type who would get jealous.

Jeff (persisting): "Richard, honest (*pause*), she's not THAT good looking, and she's really smart and a fanatic when it comes to cleaning the office...she's very organized (*pause*), and it's only for a week."

Richard: "A week?"

Larry: "Or three."

Richard admits that he could use some temporary help.

Richard reluctantly agrees to take her on and leaves. Larry and Jeff congratulate themselves for solving the problem.

10. INT. RICHARD'S HOUSE - DAY (FIVE)
Richard is talking on phone to Jeff, thanking him for the hot temp Insa while looking across his living room at her breasts (Insa is wearing a tube top). Richard remarks that she's not quite as plain-looking as Jeff had described. Richard tells Jeff that he doesn't really need office help, but Insa is helping out with housekeeping. Richard's girlfriend, Los, enters the house unannounced and demands to know who the hot temp is. Richard abruptly ends call to Jeff.

GIRLFRIEND/Los (to Richard): "WHO's the beach bunny? Are you two-timing me?"

Richard explains it's only temporary, that Insa is actually Jeff's temp and that it's short term. Los is visibly irritated when Richard tells her the hot temp's name is Insa and tells Richard off. As she leaves, she threatens repercussions if Richard doesn't get rid of 'Jugs' (*gestures towards Insa*) immediately. Richard reluctantly agrees.

11a. INT. LARRY'S OFFICE - DAY (SIX)
Larry is in his office, talking on the speakerphone to Richard about Insa. Richard apologizes for not being able to keep her.

Richard (*audio dub*): "You know (*pause*), my girlfriend, Los (*pause*), she's a clingy, needy, tri-polar HIGH maintenance broad."

Larry apologizes for not being able to take Insa back and says he only got rid her because she was causing him problems with his girlfriend.

Larry: "Yeah, Cabeca, the parts-woman I'm dating didn't want Insa around. I figured it was only temporary...just until I got Cabeca sorted out..."

Larry asks Richard how he ended up handling it.
[*SCENE TRANSITION*]

(Scene 11b - INT Richard's house)
Richard is at his desk at home, talking on the phone (handset) to Larry. Richard (*looking across the living room at Insa's breasts*) tells Larry that he didn't have the heart to fire her.

Richard: "You know the scenario, she was crying and pleading with me not to fire her because she was on a work–visa and had to be employed, and blah, blah, blah, (*pause*), I couldn't even focus on that (*pause*), by the way, did you know that 'Insa' was Bulgarian for 'Jugs'?"

Larry (*audio dub*): "Not Bulgarian, it's ROMANIAN for 'Jugs'. Apparently this is taught in grade school or something."

Richard: "Yeah, my girlfriend Los was mad as hell when I told her Insa's name."

Larry (*audio dub*): "Lost? Your girlfriends name is Lost? I thought it was Lois."

Richard: "No, it's Los, as in Los Angeles..."

Larry (*audio dub*): "Her name is Los Angeles?"

Richard: "No. Her first name is Los. Her last name is Usne."

Larry (*audio dub*): "Never mind. So, what did you do with Insa?"

Richard: "I'm having her deported" (*gazing across the living room at her breasts.*)

Larry (*audio dub*): "Deported?"

Richard: "Yeah, I called I-N-S…they'll be here any minute."

The doorbell rings (*audio dub*). Richard tells Larry to 'hold' and puts the phone down, goes to the door and lets a uniformed INS officer (Erik Estrada) in. Richard introduces the INS agent to Insa and then returns to the phone call.

Richard (to Larry): "It's all taken care of…I-N-S is here."

Larry (*audio dub*): "Is everything OK?…he's not handcuffing her or anything, is he?"

Insa can be seen/heard in the background flirting with the INS officer. The INS agent guides Insa by the arm towards the door.

INS Agent (overheard to Insa): "Don't worry, Insa, I'm SURE we can work something out. Do you like motorcycles?"

The INS Agent gives Richard a thumbs up and winks as he escorts Insa out the door.

Richard (to Larry): "Sonofabitch. I must be out of my mind…"

Richard hangs up the phone.

12. INT. LARRY'S HOUSE – DAY/NIGHT (SIX)

Larry is in his kitchen preparing for another date with Cabeca.

Larry (to Leon): "Leon, what happens to a person when they get deported?"

Leon: "How the fuck should I know? Are you gettin' deported?"

Larry: "No. Richard had to get rid of my temp, Insa. His girlfriend, Los Usne, gave him an ultimatum, and Richard didn't have the heart to fire Insa, so he had her deported."

Leon (laughing): "Los Usne?"

Larry: "Yeah, Los Usne (*pause*), that's Richard's girlfriend's name. It's a little exotic."

Leon (laughing): "LD, it's exotic alright. Los Usne is Serbian for moose lips."

Larry: "WHERE does everyone learn this stuff?"

Leon (to Larry): "You goin' out with Miss Lazy-ass parts-woman again?"

Larry: "Not lazy ass, lazy EYE (*pause*), with the wig (*pause*), and she has these fake (*pause*), what are they?

(*pause*), stick-on fingernails. She says it's low maintenance and she tells me that's what guys want--low maintenance."

Leon: "Fuck that shit, LD. You don't want LOW maintenance, you want NO maintenance."

Larry: "NO maintenance?"

Leon: "That's right. NO maintenance. Be THE MAN, LARRY, BE...THE...MAN."

Larry: "Be the man"

Leon: "I'm not FEELING it, LD --- say it like you mean it: BE (*pause*) THE (*pause*) MAN. Don't say it like a PUSSY."

Larry: "BE THE MAN."

Leon: "That's right. Women already got one pussy, they don't need another one. BE THE MAN."

Larry: "BE THE MAN."

Leon: "That's it. And remember what else I told you?"

Larry: "uhhhmmmm."

Leon: "HIT IT AND QUIT IT, LD, HIT IT AND QUIT IT."

Larry: "HIT IT AND QUIT IT."

13. EXT. STREET/PARKING - DAY/NIGHT (SIX)
Larry and Cabeca are sitting in Larry's car, parked in front of Cabeca's apartment/returning from the date. Larry is

enthusiastically kissing her, careful not to run his fingers through her long hair and instead pats her hair. Cabeca asks Larry to come upstairs for a nightcap.

14. INT. PARTS-WOMAN'S APARTMENT – DAY/NIGHT (SIX)

Larry and Cabeca are in the bedroom, sitting on the bed, (dressed), enthusiastically kissing. Cabeca asks Larry if he wants the best blowjob he will EVER have? Larry questions the use of the word 'BEST', and eventually agrees. Cabeca reaches up and takes out her (false) teeth and places them on the nightstand. Larry is stunned by the removal (*staring at the teeth*), but allows the blowjob to begin. The blowjob appears PHENOMENAL (*from facial expressions and noises*). Cabeca 'wants' Larry inside her and tells him to TAKE her from behind. Larry suggests they get undressed.

Cabeca: "Take me NOW, BIG MAN! NOW!"

Larry turns her around, approaches her and is grinding on her doggy style (both are partly undressed). A glass (marble-like) object hits the hardwood floor with a loud 'clink' noise (*audio dub*) and rolls away. Larry looks in the direction of the noise.

Larry: "What was that, it sounded like a MARBLE (*pause*), was that (*pause*), a glass eye?"
Cabeca (screaming): "KEEP going--don't stop, Larry, FUCK me, FUCK me, harder, Larry. Don't stop."

Larry hears in his head (*voice-over/audio dub*)
Leon: "HIT IT AND QUIT IT, LD."

Larry resumes action and grabs the parts-woman by the

ankle (*audio dub: loud 'Velcro rip' noise*) and a prosthetic half-leg comes off in Larry's hand. Larry looks at the leg part in his hand in horror.

Cabeca (yelling): "DON'T STOP, FUCK ME HARD, Larry...YOU'RE THE MAN."

Larry looks towards the teeth on the nightstand, then towards the glass eye on the floor and then to leg part in his hand.

Larry hears in his head (*voice-over/audio dub*)
Leon: "BE THE MAN, LD. HIT IT AND QUIT IT."

FADE OUT/Cue Music.

(END)

- 5 -

CREATIVITY – Trading the Ponies

As we noted before, ideas came to us easily. Between the lives we led and lives we were leading (in Los Angeles and Chicago), we had buckets of ideas. Turning an idea into usable material, and then into a scene or episode took at least one or two cups of coffee at a sidewalk café or a walk on the Manhattan Beach Pier.

Trading Ponies is a constant reference between us. Even this morning—which could mean the morning we wrote this or the morning you read this—it doesn't matter. If we spend any time in public, one of us will make the 'Trade a Pony' reference.

Explaining its history won't make any sense until the end of this chapter, so stick with it.

The 'Pony' part of the reference goes back to childhood Christmases. We both joked about the Christmas gifts we always wanted but never received. The grand prize of gifts for a child was a pony—which neither of us received. And how we tried: Begging, badgering, pleading, praying---the promises we made to God---it's a good thing we didn't get the ponies—we couldn't have ever lived up to those promises. We did, however, have a long list of 'booby' prizes of gifts received –slipper socks, a Chia-pet, a used encyclopedia set. What was crushing to us as kids was damned amusing to us as adults.

The 'Trade' part of the reference was purely adult. During the early part of the back-and-forth travel to Los Angeles, Ray's marriage was falling apart and John was serial dating a string of half-wits, drunks, and almost-nuns. Los Angeles, especially the beach-community area, was heaven and hell for us. Nowhere else in the world can you find a finer collection of beautiful women. They are EVERYWHERE. And they weren't afraid to 'advertise' their attributes. It has to border on cruel and unusual punishment to have us spend Monday through Friday in Los Angeles, and then come back to Chicago, in winter, and casually observe so many women that, bundled up under all the winter gear, resembled grain fed cattle….and in too many cases, resembled grain fed cattle without all the winter gear.

The combined 'Trade a Pony' reference was a corruption of the two circumstances. The first occurrence and the first one of us to utter the 'Trade a Pony' reference is lost, but the significance of it at the time was not. An absolutely stunning woman walked past us. One of us blurted out (as if praying), 'Dear Jesus….remember that pony I wanted for Christmas, but you never got for me?....I'd like to TRADE that pony and get something else………." It was a convenient and subtle code for "OH MY GOD WOULD YOU LOOK AT WHAT'S COMING UP THE SIDEWALK." And it became a running joke. One of us would make the "Dear Jesus, I'd like to trade my pony" reference and the other would shoot him down—"Nope, you already traded that pony last week, remember? No more ponies to trade." Which eventually led to a long running debate (and yes, if you're a woman and still comprehending this, *it's* completely offensive) about 'how many ponies does one get in a lifetime and how many can he trade'?

Ray wanted to date every single one of these 'ponies', but the marriage kept him from pursuing any of them. John was fooling himself with online dating sites, speed dating seminars and 'fix up' dates that belonged in asylums when he should have been chasing 'ponies'. Ray eventually got divorced. John finally listened to the advice Ray had been telling him about meeting and dating women. Accordingly, the 'Pony Trading' TOOK OFF. Would we change the past, knowing what we know now? Of course not. Well, probably not. The ideas those experiences generated were priceless*[1].

The more 'ponies' we met, the greater the realization: The new women we were encountering were nothing like the demanding princesses (ponies) we once had and traded away*[2]

Ray: I had to treat my wife like a princess….she always demanded I open ALL doors for her. We went on vacation to Fiji and I tried to open a door for her---it was on the plane while we were at 37,000 feet. She didn't go for it. **John**: Yep. I had to treat mine like a princess….I had to kneel before her---she was usually passed out on the floor when I'd come home.

These weren't fairytale princess stories with happy endings, but they did serve as creative inspiration. They were the foundation for our version of *The Princess and the*…………

---

*1 - Note to self. Send *Ex* ~~complimentary~~ C.O.D. copy of this book.

*2 - One of us really wanted to send the *Ex* to the glue factory.

Episode 3

"The Princess and the PEE"

Synopsis: Larry's attempt to live the 'Hit IT and Quit IT' lifestyle goes wrong when a speed-dating event pairs him up with a high-maintenance, demanding princess.

Scenes: 13

Cast: Larry, Leon, Jeff, misc. un-named women and men at bar, Hot woman, Obnoxious-princess woman, restaurant staff, dog pusher, dogs.

Special Guest: PGA Senior tour golfer (Fuzzy Zoeller, Lee Trevino, or Gary Player) as Leon's golf range student.

"The Princess and the PEE"

1. INT. LARRY'S HOUSE - DAY (ONE)

Larry is at home, in his bedroom, sitting on a bed. A box labeled 'Cheryl's stuff' sits in Larry's lap. Two trash bins – one labeled 'Trash', one labeled 'Recycle' stand in front of him. Larry examines the items as he removes them from the box. They are mostly 'HERS' objects from His'n'Hers sets (mugs, glasses, bowls, picture frames, a porcelain unicorn figurine). Larry looks at each object and then glances back and forth between the trash bin and the recycle bin. He gleefully tosses each item into the trash bin – breaking each piece as he disposes of it. After several items are broken, the phone rings. Larry answers. The caller is Cheryl (*voice not heard*). Leon enters the room and begins examining the items in the trash bin. Larry simultaneously waves/motions to Leon to get out while responding to (*unheard*) Cheryl on the phone. Larry says he remembers her asking for the unicorn figurine, and that he knows it was a gift from her mother, and as a coincidence, he's looking right at it (Larry peers down into the trash bin at the broken bits and the unicorn/horsehead). Larry assures Cheryl he can 'gather up' the item and bring it to her. Cheryl (*unheard*) suggests meeting in a public place—Century City Mall? Larry agrees and sets a time. Larry ends the call. Leon is still rummaging through the broken bits. Larry tells Leon to pour the pieces from the trash bin into the cardboard box and the two of them are going to the Century City Mall to meet Cheryl. Leon asks Larry if he's getting back with Cheryl.

Leon: "That's one fine ass on that woman...you mind if I hook up with her?"

Larry dismisses idea of getting back together with Cheryl. Larry says he's through with Cheryl, and that he's going after new talent.

Leon: "What new talent? You been callin' Dial-a-Ho again?"

Larry tells Leon he's going to a speed dating event the next day. Leon doesn't understand speed dating and Larry explains it.

Larry: "You get the maximum return on your investment. No spending an entire evening with one woman. Five minutes. That's all. Five minutes and you decide...and then move on to the next...it's kind of the middle-aged-white-guy's version of what you are always telling me: 'Hit It and Quit It'."

Leon: "Now you're talking my vernacular, LD."

Larry: "Vernacular??"

2. INT. SHOPPING MALL – DAY (ONE)
Larry and Leon are walking through a shopping mall. Leon wants to stop for food. Larry insists on getting to the meeting-spot with Cheryl on-time. Leon points out a fast-food restaurant, tells Larry he will catch up with him at the meeting spot, and walks away. Larry arrives at the meeting spot (fountain/center court/seating area). Larry takes a seat and repeatedly/alternates checking his watch and his cellphone. Leon reappears carrying a take-out tray of food and 2 large drink bottles (vitamin water) and gives one to Larry. Larry accepts, guzzles half the bottle and continues checking his watch and cellphone. Larry becomes irritated, remarking to Leon that Cheryl is always late. Larry says

that he won't wait any longer and they are leaving.
Leon complains that he hasn't finished his snack. Larry tells Leon to dump it as he picks up the box. They both walk towards a row of trash bins. Standing in front of the bins, they look at the bins and then at each other – perplexed. There are 10 bins, each labeled differently – Glass, Plastic, Paper, Liquids, Metals, Non-recyclable, Pet Waste, Diapers, Syringes, Compost. Each has a narrow opening preventing large items from being inserted.

Leon (to Larry): "Whodafuck put compost in a shoppin' mall???"

Larry puts Cheryl's box on top of the pet waste bin.

Leon: "Pet waste???"

Larry: "It was a Unicorn...that's an animal."

Leon forces his food tray into the syringes bin and asks Larry if he's just going to leave the box. Larry tells Leon he will send Cheryl a text message telling her where to find it and that way she can't blame him if the item is broken when she finds the box. Larry (holding his water bottle) and Leon walk away.

3. EXT. LARRY'S CAR, LEAVING SHOPPING MALL PARKING LOT – DAY (ONE)
Larry and Leon are in traffic. Larry tells Leon he doesn't want to ruin the day after wasting time at the mall and suggests going to the driving range. Larry calls Jeff from his cell phone and invites him to meet them at the golf range. Jeff agrees and they set a time. Larry tells Jeff he has to stop at his house and pick up his clubs first. Larry

ends the call. Larry continues to gulp from the drink bottle and returns it to the cup holder in the center console.

4. INT-EXT. WALKING INTO GOLF COURSE-DRIVING RANGE – DAY (ONE)

Larry and Leon are inside the driving range pro shop getting clubs for Leon and range balls. Leon (wearing a scotch plaid shirt) picks up a golfers cap and two drink bottles and tells the cashier to add it to the tab. Larry picks up a bucket of balls, one drink bottle and heads towards the driving range. Leon follows carrying clubs. Leon, walking out to the driving range with the bags is mistaken for a caddie by another golfer (special guest, Fuzzy Zoeller) who tells Leon to take his clubs out to his car. Leon goes off on the golfer.

Leon: "Not all black people are caddies….a lot of them may drive a CADDY but that don't make them no fuckin' CADDIE….I'm a GOLFIN' PRO…see THE hat?"

The golfer apologizes and asks if Leon can give him some golf pointers. Leon tells him it will be COSTLY.

Leon: "Show me SOME LETTUCE."

The golfer pulls out a stack of bills, Leon gestures towards the tees and they walk off. Jeff arrives and walks towards Larry as Leon and the golfer walk past. Jeff looks, says 'hello' to Leon, and keeps walking. Leon is heard saying that was one of his former students on the BGA - 'the BIG Golfers Association'.

5. INT. INSIDE DRIVING RANGE/GOLF COURSE CLUBHOUSE – DAY (ONE)

Larry is talking to Jeff, returning to the clubhouse from the driving range. Larry is wondering/asking where Leon is. Larry tells Jeff that Cheryl blew him off for their meeting at the mall. Jeff asks if Larry is trying to get back together with her. Larry dismisses the idea, says that he's through with Cheryl, and that he's going to a speed dating event the next day. Jeff doesn't understand speed dating and Larry explains it.

Larry: "You get maximum return on your investment. No spending an entire evening with one woman. Five minutes. That's all. Five minutes and you decide: 'Keep or Toss', and then move on to the next woman."

Jeff: "Five minutes??? Keep or Toss??? AND move on???...I'd like to do that with Susie."

Leon appears, counting money.

Larry: "Where'd that come from?"

Leon: "Just givin' my man over there some golf tips."

Larry: "Tips? You've never even had a golf club in your hands before today."

Leon's golf student approaches Leon, thanks him for the instruction, and hands him a cash tip. Larry and Jeff stare in disbelief.

Larry: "I gotta take a leak---those vitamin waters run right through me."

6. INT. INSIDE RESTAURANT-BANQUET AREA FOR SPEED DATING EVENT – DAY/NIGHT (TWO)

Larry surveys the speed dating seminar room as he sips from a half-full bottle of vitamin water. A long row of tables are set up with men on one side, women on the other. An announcement is made and the event begins. Larry takes a seat to start his first session. The woman on the opposite side of the table has a blank, expressionless stare and replies with nods and 'yes' or 'no', regardless of what Larry says. The session completes. Larry stands, turns to leave and pauses.

Larry (to woman across from him): "Have a nice life…or death…or whatever state you're in."

Larry moves down one seat and begins the next session. The woman across from him is a 'close talker' and leans in to Larry's face to speak to him. Larry leans back to create space and the woman leans in further to maintain uncomfortable closeness. The session completes. Larry stands, turns to leave and pauses. Larry pulls a single Tic-tac candy from his pocket, places it on the table and slides it towards the woman.

Larry moves to the next seat and begins the next session. The woman across from him is a 'long talker'. As Larry is introducing himself, the long-talker interrupts him and talks nonstop, bringing inappropriate topics into her constant stream (mother has uterine cancer, ex-husband 'went' gay, cousin was a prostitute, but only as a way to support her drug habit, etc.). Larry notices an incredibly attractive (HOT) woman down the line and makes eye contact, smiles, and nods at her while tolerating the long talker. The long talker, droning on, remarks: 'small bladders run in my family.' On hearing the small bladder remark, Larry jumps up, interrupts the long-talker to tell her he has the same small bladder condition and has to go. Larry begins walking toward the restroom. Mentally/talking to himself, he 'calculates' how to time his pee break so that he gets back just in time to sit with the HOT woman.

Larry (to himself): "Let's see...I can pee in 90 seconds, but the attractive woman is 1 seat away...which is...ummmm, 5 minutes...plus the remainder of this session, plus the delay between the session...ugghh this is highschool algebra all over again. Two trains leave their stations at the same time. Aggghhhh"

7. INT. INSIDE RESTAURANT – STANDING OUTSIDE RESTROOM DOOR – DAY/NIGHT (TWO)

Larry tries the Men's room door knob, finds it occupied /locked, and waits. He glances at his watch, and says/asks himself, 'I wonder if I have time to take a degner?' Larry looks at his watch and looks over to the open Ladies restroom door, to the Men's restroom door, to a nearby sink, to bucket on the floor, and back to the Men's room door; Larry rattles the Men's room doorknob again, and a voice is heard (*audio dub*): 'I'm IN HERE.' Larry decides (*talking to himself*) he cannot wait. Larry enters the Ladies restroom and closes the door (and relieves himself). As Larry opens the door to exit the Ladies restroom, the close-talker (*visibly irritated*) is standing/waiting for the Ladies room. She leans in (*too close*) and gives Larry a nasty scowl.

Close Talker: "THIS is the Ladies room."

Larry: "YES. Yes, it is. Try the complimentary mouthwash."

Larry sidesteps around her and walks back toward the speed dating tables.

8. INT. INSIDE RESTAURANT-BANQUET AREA FOR SPEED DATING EVENT – DAY/NIGHT (TWO)

Larry returns to the tables but has missed his turn/session with the HOT woman –the seat across from her is occupied, but the next seat in line is open. Larry takes the open seat and talks to the woman across the table while staring at the HOT woman. The HOT woman smiles back at Larry. The woman talking to Larry is a 'princess' type. The princess talks intelligently with Larry, makes it obvious she likes him and suggests they go out on a longer date. An announcement is made that the event is over. Larry (*reluctantly*) agrees to go on a date with the princess and she gives him her contact info on a scrap of paper. The Hot woman observes Larry taking the phone number from the princess and leaves – Larry does not realize the HOT woman has left.

9. EXT. PUBLIC PARK, OUTDOOR CONCESSION AREA WITH TABLES AND CHAIRS – DAY (THREE)

Larry and Leon are in a public park concession area sitting and opening bottles of vitamin water. Larry is talking about the upcoming date with the princess woman he met at the speed dating seminar. Larry has no enthusiasm for the date and regrets letting the HOT woman slip away. As Larry is talking, a woman approaches the next table pushing a baby stroller. Larry smiles at her and looks in the stroller. The woman has a tiny dog in the seat. The woman places the tiny dog on the ground and places a small bowl with the name 'Cheryl' on it next to the dog and fills it with a bottle of vitamin water. Leon tells Larry that he MUST go through with THE date. It's Larry's obligation to try to TAP the princess, even if he doesn't like her. While Leon is talking, the small dog pisses a large quantity on the ground and a dog-piss river forms, heading towards Larry's shoes, forming a puddle under Larry. Larry does not notice. He and Leon get up and walk away (*sipping from bottles of vitamin water*). Larry senses something on the bottom of his shoe and looks/drags the shoe on the ground to clean it, while remarking that he must have stepped in something. Larry and Leon continue walking-talking-sipping. Larry spots the HOT woman from the speed dating event walking a dog in the park. Larry points out the HOT woman to Leon. Leon tells Larry she's FINE and if Larry doesn't put THE moves on her right now, he will. Larry approaches the HOT woman. They chat about the speed dating event. The HOT woman's dog becomes excited after sniffing the dog piss on Larry's shoes and pees on Larry's leg. The HOT woman is embarrassed and apologizes. She takes out a scrap of paper, uses lipstick to write her name and number on it and gives it to Larry. She tells Larry to call her—she'll take care of the cleaning bill and make it up to him. Larry flashes the paper at Leon. Leon makes an obscene gesture and nods approval back at Larry. Larry promises to call her and they part. Larry and Leon walk to Larry's car in the parking lot. Larry places the paper on the dash of his car, reaches for the seatbelt, buckles it and begins to drive away. The scrap of paper floats off the dash into the console-cupholder (*unnoticed*).

10. EXT. DRIVEWAY IN FRONT OF PRINCESS WOMAN'S HOUSE – DAY/NIGHT (THREE)
Larry pulls into the driveway of the princess woman's

house for their date. Larry takes a final swig from a bottle of vitamin water before getting out of the car and places the empty bottle in the console (*covering the scrap paper with the HOT woman's phone number*). Larry approaches the front door and rings the bell. The princess-woman (*wearing a 'busy' dress with white gloves*) answers the door (*only opening it slightly*) and does not invite Larry in. She opens the door further and as Larry moves forward she exits, pushing him back and closes the door. They walk to Larry's car. Larry is seated in the car when he realizes she's standing at the passenger door. Larry yells to her 'it's open', but she doesn't move. Larry realizes she's waiting for him to open the door. Larry gets out, walks around the car, opens the door for her, closes it, sighs, walks back to his side and gets in.

11. EXT. RESTAURANT PARKING LOT – DAY/NIGHT (THREE)

Larry parks the car in a spot between two other cars at the restaurant. Larry gets out and walks to the end of the car. He presses the remote to lock the car before looking back and realizing the princess woman is still in the car (*waiting for Larry to open her door*). Larry goes back to open her door, has to fumble with the remote, and opens the car door for her (rolling his eyes *and nodding his head*).

12. EXT-INT. RESTAURANT FRONT DOOR/INSIDE OF RESTAURANT – DAY/NIGHT (THREE)

Larry approaches the restaurant door and walks through the door first. The princess woman stands outside waiting, refusing to hold the open door for herself. Larry goes back out the door, holds it open and follows her in. A waiter immediately takes them to a table. Larry sits, while the princess woman stands waiting. The waiter pulls out the chair for her and seats her.

Princess woman (to the waiter): "MY...SUCH a GENTLEMAN. It's a shame there are SO few of you left."

The dinner conversation between Larry and the princess woman is awkward. The princess woman complains of a draft and Larry offers her his jacket. Larry repeatedly checks his watch and gulps a LARGE glass of wine.

Larry (*audio dub voiceover, in his head*): "WHEN will this nightmare end?"

Following dinner, the waiter approaches and offers the princess woman the dessert menu. Larry declines dessert for both of them and requests the check. The waiter replies that he does not have it and will have to retrieve it.

Larry: "A GENTLEMAN would retrieve it as soon as possible."

The princess woman drones on (slow-motion, clear words are not heard). The waiter returns with the dinner check. Larry throws an excessive amount of cash on the table, tells the princess woman he always tips BIG, pulls her chair back and hustles her out of the restaurant and to his car, opening/holding doors for her all the way.

13. EXT. DRIVEWAY IN FRONT OF PRINCESS WOMAN'S HOUSE – DAY/NIGHT (THREE)
Larry and the princess woman arrive at her home. Larry parks in the driveway near the street (*10 different*

trash/recycle bins can be seen on the curb). Larry jumps out and walks to the passenger side to open the car door.

Larry *(audio dub voiceover, in his head)*: "I should have used the bathroom at the restaurant..."

Larry walks the princess woman to her front door and advises that he has to pee and asks to use her bathroom. The princess woman refuses. The princess woman (still wearing Larry's jacket) opens door slightly, slips through the narrow opening and abruptly closes the door in Larry's face. Larry is still asking to use her bathroom. Larry walks to his car, looking around for a tree or shrub to use. As Larry returns to his car, he notices the empty vitamin water bottle in the console and retrieves it. Larry glances up and down the deserted street and uses the bottle as a urinal, standing in front of his car to hide from passers-by. Larry finishes and replaces the cap on the bottle. Larry looks at the variety of trash containers and can't decide which container to place the bottle. The princess woman comes out of her house walking rapidly towards Larry (holding Larry's jacket). Larry tosses the full bottle under his car and leaps in. Larry starts his car, puts it in reverse, and starts backing out of the driveway. (*Camera close up: The bottle has rolled under the passenger side wheel.*) The princess woman stands outside the passenger door, waiting. Larry refuses to get out, and lowers the passenger window. The princess woman flings Larry's jacket through the window and makes a rude comment about Larry not being a gentleman. Larry turns/looks out rear window and resumes backing out of driveway. The car tire crushes the bottle of urine. The bottle bursts and blasts the princess with pee. Larry hears a gasp, looks across the dashboard through the passenger window at the dripping-wet princess woman. His eye catches the now-visible scrap of paper with the HOT Woman's name and phone number. Larry faintly smiles and drives off.

FADE OUT/Cue Music.

(END)

EDITING – Tense and Tension

In terms of writing --- in the sense of forming an idea, building it into a concept, and telling it to each other, we (Ray and John) are, in gentleman's terms: Genius. From the smallest spark – standing in the aisle of an airplane waiting to get into the airport generated the idea for a complete episode ('Hairs Looking at You') to real life experiences (the women we were dating in LA forming the basis for the 'Ms. Potatohead' episode), we found inspiration everywhere. Building it into a storyline and telling each other wasn't so much a business process as just getting a laugh from each other.

If we had the foresight to write it down, even if it were only to scribble some notes on the back of a menu or a napkin, and made it into our written ideas list spreadsheet, it was still a long way from becoming usable material. One of us, usually the one who first created the idea or concept, would write the outline. We tested several formats, starting with a generic version, and eventually used a format that was already well defined. We had copies of pages from various TV sitcom scripts, including actual Curb Your Enthusiasm outlines. We already knew the types of characters we wanted to create, so we built a template file in a word processor application. Just 'fill-in-the-blanks'. What could be simpler? Answer: Anything and EVERYTHING, it turns out.

John: Ray's command of language and grammar is actually quite good. His way to apply it: quite bad. Ray would write entire episodes and change the 'tense' from PRESENT, to FUTURE to PAST tense within the space of a few scenes...or even a few lines.

This would drive me UP THE F**KING WALL. It was worse when the variation took place several scenes apart. Editing Rays work *always* took longer than putting the original idea onto paper. As if that weren't enough, Ray had (has!) a tendency for dreaming up better ideas: "what if we ……" Without a firm 'NO' from me, some of the episodes printed in this book (and even this paragraph) would STILL be in re-write.

Ray: John, on the other hand, usually edited his work to a high degree before passing it to me for review. Unfortunately, John managed to edit a lot of the humor right out of the scenes and ideas. Suggestions that I had previously rattled off were forgotten or misinterpreted or just poorly executed. And this, naturally, would drive me, UP THE F**KING WALL. Restoring the humor to John's work *always* took longer than putting the original idea onto paper. As if that weren't enough, John had (has!) this inexplicable drive to put a hook or common thread in every episode, and slip it into subsequent episodes. "Let's use the term xxxxxx in this scene." Without a firm 'NO' from me, some of the episodes printed in this book (and the previous paragraph) would be FILLED with nonsensical references.

Fortunately, moderation and compromise were easy to come by between us. Our formula to writing always included some 'shelf time'. We would take whatever suggestions the other had, incorporate as best as possible and then put the episode aside for a few days or even weeks. When we came back to it, either it was pure genius or the guilty party saw the error and conceded. Proof that *Good Things Come to Those Who*……

Episode 4

"Good Things Come to Those Who Weigh(t)"

Synopsis: Larry's tries to help Jeff lose weight by hiring a celebrity personal trainer for him. The trainer turns Jeff's life into a 24x7 nightmare when he moves in with Jeff and his wife.

Scenes: 15

Cast: Larry, Jeff, Susie, Leon, Richard Lewis, Antoinette, misc. birthday guests, misc. HBO office executives, restaurant staff, policewoman, and random child.

Special Guest: Richard Simmons as himself.

"Good Things Come to Those Who Weigh(t)"

1. EXT. COUNTRY CLUB GOLF COURSE, 1st TEE – DAY (ONE)

Larry and Jeff are on a golf course – Jeff is bending down to place the ball on the tee and makes a grunting noise. As he stands upright, the ball immediately falls off the tee. Jeff complains about his belly and how he can't lose weight – he attempts to tee up the ball again (*grunting*) and splits/rips the seat of his pants (*audio dub: rip noise*). Jeff mentions to Larry all the diets he's tried.

Jeff: "ALL of them…Atkins, WeightWatchers, South Beach, South Bitch…"

Larry: "South Bitch?"

Jeff: "Susie nagged me while she vacationed in Miami Beach. None of these diets work."

Jeff (in a disgusted tone): "Susie is right…I AM A FAT Fuck."

Larry ponders the 'fat fuck' comment but agrees Jeff could lose a few pounds. Jeff hits the ball off the tee and slices it into the woods. Larry asks if he wants to tee up another shot. Jeff stares at the tee for a long moment.

Jeff: "Too much work…I'll take a drop."

2. INT. COUNTRY CLUB LOCKER ROOM – DAY (ONE)

Larry and Jeff are changing back into street clothes. Jeff compliments Larry on his incredible game. Larry says he was feeling good and felt really loose. Jeff is disgusted with his game and states if he doesn't lose weight, he's giving up golf. Jeff tells Larry he's supposed to weigh himself to keep track of his weight. A scale is visible near a door marked 'Toilet' in the locker-room. Jeff moves towards the scale and then stops. Larry looks up.

Jeff: "Wait...I'll lighten the load first."

Larry looks puzzled. Jeff reaches for the door marked 'Toilet'.

Jeff: "I'm gonna take a degner first, that should be good for at least a pound."

Larry nods in agreement.

3. EXT. EXITING COUNTRY CLUB/CLUBHOUSE –DAY (ONE)
Larry and Jeff are leaving the clubhouse. A young boy is selling chocolate cupcakes in the parking lot.

Boy (to Jeff/Larry): "Excuse me sir, would you like to help out the McMutton School of Arts and buy some GREAT chocolate cupcakes?"

Larry (to Jeff): "Did he say he was selling mutton?"

Jeff (looking interested) pulls out his wallet.
(**Susie *voiceover*,** with a 'pop-up' onscreen image of Susie giving him a dirty look and waving her finger back and forth at him: "You....fat... fuck"). Jeff steps back.
Jeff (politely) to the boy: "No, thanks...chocolate causes me (pause) hallucinations."

Larry has already pulled out a $5 bill and is giving it to the boy. The boy gives Larry a jumbo cupcake in a clear plastic box. Jeff is staring intensely at the box. Larry and Jeff walk toward their cars.

Jeff: "Ya wanna share that?"

Larry: "It won't help your golf game."

4. INT. LARRY'S HOUSE – DAY (ONE)
Larry (walking towards the kitchen) greets Leon and proceeds to the answering machine and presses the 'Play' button. The answering machine plays the 'intro' using a (new) greeting from LEON. Larry looks at Leon with a puzzled look. Messages begin to play. Message after message (all female callers), are for Leon. Larry says he has not received a message in quite some time and now he knows why.

Leon: "I had to erase your messages because the voicemail box was full and I didn't want to miss any calls from da bitches."

Larry looks astonished and nods in disbelief. Leon recalls/tells Larry that there was a message from Susie...something about Jeff's birthday coming up and getting a gift for Jeff. Leon moves to the living room. He picks up the TV remote and begins flipping through TV channels.

Larry (talking to himself): "Jeff's birthday...I need to get him something....Leon, what can I get Jeff?"

Leon replies with two or three far-fetched ideas---get him

an 8-ball---get him a hooker, etc. Leon (still flipping TV channels) complains that Larry needs to get some titty-channels. Leon says he's tired of the same boring channels...'Home Shopping, news, weather and exercise shit!' Leon flips past a Richard Simmons workout program.

Larry: "Wait...Wait...Go Back!"

Leon goes back to the Richard Simmons program - the 'high intensity, calorie burning workout show.' The program is just finishing.

Leon: "That's one pretty insane fucked-up dude...all sweaty and shit!"

Larry: "Yeah...Pretty, Pretty, Pretty, Good..."

5. EXT. LARRY, DRIVING IN HIS CAR – DAY (TWO)
Larry, using his cell phone, calls his office. Antoinette answers and Larry asks if he has any messages. Antoinette responds with 'none that I recall.' Larry asks Antoinette to get him the contact information for Richard Simmons.

Antoinette: "Who?"

Larry: "You know...that guy with the big hair and cute shorts...The EXERCISE guy!"

Larry makes questionable hand gestures inside his car for 'cute' and 'exercise' and looks out the passenger window (waiting at red light) - a hefty policewoman in a police car is eating a Twinkie with crumbs/cream stuck on her chin. She glares at Larry. Antoinette questions Larry on why he needs the information?

Larry: "Never mind...It's for a friend...Just GET ME the information (looking at the policewoman). I gotta go!"

Larry ends the call.

6. INT. LARRY'S OFFICE – DAY (TWO)
Larry walks in the office. Antoinette (on the phone) hands a piece of paper to Larry. Larry examines it. It's the Richard Simmons information. Larry says he is impressed with how fast she obtained the contact information and gives Antoinette the 'thumbs up'. Antoinette (still on phone, covering the mouthpiece) waves Larry away. Larry asks Antoinette who she's talking to: 'is THAT HIM on the phone?' (*Larry leans in, close to the earpiece/Antoinette's head, to listen/hear who's on the line*).

Antoinette (pulls the phone away): "EXCUSE me...it's NONE of your business...it's a friend."

Larry proceeds into his office, sits down, dials the phone number and asks for Richard.

Larry: "Richard?...Larry David...Larry David...yes, David is my last name......yeah, very clever Richard, two first names, that's right. Listen, Richard..."
[*Fade out*]

7. INT. JEFF AND SUSIE'S HOUSE –DAY (THREE)
A crowd of people are in Jeff's kitchen finishing the 'Happy Birthday' song.

Jeff (standing in front of a cake): "I wish (pause)."
Jeff looks at Susie and blows out the candles.

Jeff: "This chocolate cake looks FABULOUS. Just the other day, I turned away some kid selling chocolate cupcakes only because I didn't want to spoil my anticipation for my birthday cake. I'm going to make-up for it by having a king-sized piece."

Jeff proceeds to cut the cake. All the slices are small except for a purposely cut king-sized piece he keeps for himself. Jeff is holding his plate in one hand and a large chunk of cake on the fork in the other. He prepares to take the first big bite (bringing the fork up to his open mouth), as the doorbell rings. Jeff pauses and gives a puzzled look.

Larry (mocking): "I wonder who that can be? Perhaps a strip-o-gram?"

Jeff heads (*quickly*) to the door and opens it (*the crowd follows him to the door*). Richard Simmons appears, holding a large suitcase and a small but overweight dog on a leash dressed just like Richard (tight red & white striped short shorts). The dog turns/shifts a little to expose his sagging balls that are hanging out of the dog shorts. Richard hands Larry the large suitcase and the dog on a leash.

Richard Simmons (yells): "Happy Birthday, Jeffrey!" (*gives Jeff an enthusiastic hug.*)

Jeff stares at Richard Simmons (*still holding the plate/cake, mouth hanging open, as if in shock*). Richard takes the plate with the large piece of chocolate cake from Jeff's hand, and says how excited he is to be here.

Richard Simmons: "The party starts now!"

Larry explains his gift of 'Richard Simmons' to Jeff and says that this is his answer to Jeff's birthday wish.

Jeff (interrupts Larry): "My Birthday wish wasn't to lose weight, I wished I would lose (pause) Susie." (*Susie scowls and/or curses at Jeff.*)

Larry: "You have a FULL week with Richard Simmons...7 FULL days. Not only will you lose weight but this will improve your golf game. Happy Birthday."

Richard Simmons: "That's RIGHT, Jeffrey. You may be a TON of fun now, but we'll make you just a few pounds of fun in no time."

Susie (in background) remarks excitedly about finally seeing Jeff lose weight. She greets Richard Simmons.

Susie: "Let me show you to your room Richard!...Larry...do something with THAT (*pointing to Richard Simmons' pudgy dog*) and bring up Richard's luggage!...Hurry up...make yourself useful!"

8. INT. JEFF AND SUSIE'S HOUSE –DAY/NIGHT (THREE)

Jeff is lying in bed, wide awake, staring at the ceiling, his stomach making loud noises. Susie is snoring/sound asleep. Jeff slips out of bed quietly and leaves the bedroom.

[*SCENE TRANSITION*]

Jeff is quietly moving down the stairs and goes to the kitchen. Jeff walks up to the refrigerator, pauses, looks left and right, opens the door slowly/quietly and focuses on his uneaten piece of chocolate birthday cake. Jeff gazes 'lovingly' at the cake. The cake appears to 'sparkle' (*special effects*). Jeff licks his lips and reaches for the plate. As he closes the refrigerator door, Richard Simmons is standing there shaking his head in disappointment. Richard Simmons takes the cake out of Jeff's hands, puts it back into the refrigerator, and pulls out a celery stalk.

Richard Simmons (waving the celery stalk at Jeff): "6am. WE start our workout!" Richard hands the celery to Jeff.

Jeff glances over at the pudgy sleeping dog, its balls draped out. Jeff takes a bite out of the celery stalk, makes a frustrated face, spits the celery in the trash and heads back upstairs.

9. INT. JEFF AND SUSIE'S HOUSE – DAY (FOUR)
An alarm clock (showing 5:30AM) next to Jeff's bed beeps. Jeff struggles to get up and out of bed.

[*SCENE TRANSITION*]

Jeff (*approaching the kitchen*), is dressed in workout attire (*appears really sleepy*). Richard Simmons is in the kitchen, wide awake with a healthy breakfast plate prepared. Richard greets Jeff with an overly cheery, 'good morning, sunshine.' Jeff grunts and makes his way to the refrigerator. Jeff opens the refrigerator and the piece of chocolate cake is calling out to him.
(*Sexy woman's voiceover:* "Jeff. TAKE ME, Jeff. You know you want me. TAKE ME. Take ALL of me.")
After a long stare, Jeff removes a bottle of orange juice and

pours a glass. Jeff sits down at the table (half asleep), eating unenthusiastically/un-motivated from the plate prepared by Richard. Richard Simmons is loudly and excitedly talking non-stop about their daily workout agenda.

10. EXT. YARD OR PUBLIC PARK – DAY (FOUR)

Jeff is doing 'Jumping Jacks' (sweating profusely, huffing and puffing).

Richard Simmons (upbeat–shouting): "Alright! Alright…almost done…let's go…squeeze that tushy!"

Jeff glares at him. Jeff finishes his last of 50 'Jumping Jacks' (counts: "49"…"50").

Richard Simmons: "Next, we do Belly Buster Sit-ups. Sit-ups, sit-ups and more sit-ups!"

Jeff: "I haven't done a sit-up since high school."

Richard Simmons (quick retort): "I can see that, pork chop!"

Richard lies on a workout mat and tells Jeff to hold his feet down so he can show Jeff the perfect sit-up. Jeff, holding his feet notices Richard Simmons is wearing no underwear. Jeff sees what appear to be Richard's balls hanging out of his red & white striped short shorts. Jeff makes a disgusted face, turns and looks away.

Richard Simmons: "Pay attention, fat boy. There's no salami hiding in there…..I can't stress how important this is!"

Jeff: "Salami?"

Jeff forces himself to pay attention (cringing face).

11. INT. JEFF AND SUSIE'S HOUSE – DAY (FOUR)
Jeff is dressed in a suit and tells Susie he's leaving for the office. Susie gives Jeff an up-and-down sexy look-over…checks him out and gives Jeff an approving nod and smile. Richard Simmons (happy and upbeat) gives Jeff some words of encouragement and a big hug before Jeff walks out the door. During the hug, Richard feels something pressing up against him coming from Jeff's pants pocket ('What's this?'). Richard Simmons reaches into Jeff's pants pocket, feels around and pulls out a candy bar. Richard gives a big disappointed look to Jeff. Jeff glances at Susie, (shaking her head in disappointment at Jeff).

Susie (to Richard Simmons): "You better keep a close eye on that!" (*pointing to Jeff.*)

12. INT. RESTAURANT TABLE – DAY (FIVE)
Larry, Jeff and Richard Simmons are having lunch/finishing their meals. Richard Simmons' cell phone rings and he excuses himself from the table to take the call. Jeff vents to Larry about the hell he's going through with Richard Simmons and how it's like boot camp…even worse! Jeff talks about the dog --- how it eats, shits and sleeps all day and how his balls hang out of the undersized doggy shorts. Jeff tells Larry how he had to hold Richard Simmons' ankles as he was demonstrating sit-ups and how he wears no underwear and his balls were hanging out.

Jeff: "It's one big ball festival at my house! He keeps saying things like, 'there's no Salami hiding in there.' WHAT the fuck is that supposed to mean?"

Larry (barely paying attention to Jeff) is looking at the dessert menu and comments on the dessert specials.

Larry: "Chocolate mousse cake...that's my favorite. Salami? What's that supposed to mean?"

Richard Simmons returns from his phone call.

Larry: "Hey Richard...dessert?"

Richard Simmons says he's stuffed and won't be ordering dessert and excuses himself once again to use 'the little boy's room.' Richard walks away and waitress arrives to ask if they saved room for dessert.

Jeff: "I'm starving–my entire lunch was the equivalent of a celery stalk and soda cracker. Third-world prisoners eat better than this."

Larry (looking at Jeff, puzzled expression): "Salami?...I'll have the chocolate mousse cake special."

Jeff: "I'd like that too (*groans*), but I'll have the low-cal fruit plate."

While waiting for the dessert, Jeff comments to Larry that they are cutting it close to their after-lunch appointment at HBO. Jeff tells Larry that Susie gave him a 'sexy look' before leaving for work and how he has not had that look in ages. Jeff's eyes immediately catch the attention of an attractive female customer passing by their table. Jeff makes eye contact, smiles, says 'hello' and turns his head to watch her strut past.

Jeff (to Larry): "What was I just saying?"
Larry (also watching the female customer leave): "Something about salami."

The waitress arrives with the dessert plates. The waitress accidentally gives the low-cal fruit plate to Larry and the (oversized) chocolate mousse cake to Jeff. Before the plates can be switched, Jeff quickly grabs his fork, shoves it in the cake and carves off a big piece. As the fork reaches his (*open*) mouth, Richard Simmons (*from off camera*) appears at the table and sees Jeff with the big bite of cake on his fork. Jeff's eyes meet Richards' (*long pause, Jeff sighs, looking guilty*). Richard (*mouth wide open in shock*) shakes his head and tells Jeff he is extremely disappointed. Jeff tries to explain how the waitress screwed up the desserts and how he ordered the low-cal fruit plate and NOT the chocolate cake and he was just having 'a taste'.

Richard Simmons (shouting): "You expect me to believe that? Give me 20 deep-knee bends. Right now."

Jeff: "Here?"

Richard Simmons (shouting): "Would you like to make it 30? NOW!"

Jeff stands up, groans and in front of the restaurant customers begins exercising.

Jeff: "One"…"Two"…"Three…"

As Jeff does the exercises, Larry switches dessert plates, and enthusiastically eats the mousse cake.

13. INT. HBO OFFICE CONFERENCE ROOM – DAY (FIVE)

A group of HBO executives are sitting around a conference room table discussing details of a potential business deal with Jeff and Larry. The camera slowly pans around the table, past the HBO executives, to Larry, and to Jeff. Richard Simmons is seen sitting away from the table, against a wall in a conference room chair. Richard is sitting straight up, hands folded, with perfect posture. Jeff looks at a large bowl of candy in the middle of the conference room table and then glances over at Richard. They make eye contact. Richard is motioning for Jeff to suck in his stomach. The HBO executives notice the gesturing and stop talking.

HBO executives: "Why is Richard Simmons here?"

Jeff looks at Larry. Larry raises his hands/nods (*as if to say he has no part of it*).

Jeff (hesitantly): "It's for medical reasons…that I can't discuss."

Larry nods in agreement/approval. Jeff revives the conversation about the potential project and then excuses himself to use the facilities.

[71]

14. INT. OUTSIDE/AT DOOR OF HBO CONFERENCE ROOM – DAY (FIVE)

Jeff exits the conference room closing the door behind him. Jeff walks across a hallway to the vending machines, peers through the glass (*like a kid in a candy store*), makes 'mmmmm' sounds, and focuses on a favorite.

Jeff: "Ahhh, the good old standby…chocolate-covered nutlog…C18."

Jeff steps back and reaches for his wallet. While searching for a dollar bill, an office worker cuts in front of him, inserts a bill into the machine, and lingers over a selection.

Jeff (anxious/pleads to office worker): "kinda in a hurry here…"

The office worker gives a rude look to Jeff and chooses (*announces out loud*) 'C18' (the same candy bar Jeff was eyeing)—slowly pressing the vending machine numbers

Office worker: "C………1………8."

The machine makes noises. The candy bar is 'STUCK'/hanging and does not fall. The office worker swears at the machine, shakes the machine, pounds on it, etc. The candy bar will not drop. The office worker reaches back into his pocket for another dollar bill but has no small bills. The office worker turns to Jeff and asks him if he can change a twenty dollar bill.

Jeff (holding a dollar in his hand): "Sorry, I only have hundreds."

The office worker (*scowling/visibly frustrated*) leaves. Jeff receives a text on his cell phone from Richard Simmons.

Jeff (reading the message aloud): "WHERE ARE You??? ...Richard."

Jeff (nodding): "I'll tell you WHERE I'm at." (*Jeff presses the DELETE button.*)

Jeff looks back at the machine (*excited/mumbling*).

Jeff: "SCORE.... 2 for 1."

Jeff puts a dollar in the machine. Jeff's arm extends to make his selection.

Jeff: "C18...C... 1..."

Just as Jeff's finger reaches the 8 button (*from off camera*), Richard Simmons' hand reaches in and presses the #9. The vending machine drops down a bag of carrots. Jeff looks up in startled horror (*Richard Simmons is standing next to him*). Richard voices disappointment and disapproval with Jeff.

Richard Simmons (yelling): "TWO CANDYBARS? ...TWO??...DOUBLE THE FAT."

Jeff (interrupting Richard Simmons): "NO...NO...there was another guy buying the candy bar and it got stuck!"

Richard Simmons (mocking) looks around for the other person and looks back at Jeff in disbelief.

Richard Simmons: "DOUBLE THE PUNISHMENT! GIVE ME 40!"

Jeff, without hesitation, begins doing jumping jacks. While Jeff is doing the reps, Larry & the HBO executives crowd the doorway of the conference room—peering at the vending area. Larry walks across the hallway to the vending machine, takes a dollar out, puts it in the machine and presses #C18. The TWO candy bars drop. Larry removes both and starts eating one. Larry suggests they adjourn the meeting for the day and resume *(pauses, looks at Jeff and then at Richard)*: 'in a week or so.' The HBO executives agree and leave. Jeff finishes the exercise and scowls at Richard. Larry and Jeff talk briefly and decide to go straight to Jeff's house and create a plan for next week's meeting.

15. EXT. JEFF'S HOUSE – DRIVEWAY – DAY (FIVE)
Larry drives up/arrives at Jeff's house before Jeff and Richard Simmons.

[*SCENE TRANSITION*]

Larry enters the kitchen, glances around, goes to the refrigerator and takes out (Jeff's) leftover chocolate birthday cake and picks up a fork. Larry's cell phone rings (*audio dub*) just as he is bringing the fork to his (open) mouth. Larry answers his phone. Jeff is calling, asking Larry if he's at the house (*audio dub*). Larry acknowledges and Jeff asks Larry to look for his sunglasses in his den/office. Larry places the cake on the kitchen table, and walks away (talking to Jeff on the phone). Richard Simmons' dog appears in the kitchen as Larry exits. The dog eats part of the slice of cake and makes belching noises (*audio dub*).

[*SCENE TRANSITION*]

Jeff and Richard drive up/arrive home.

[*SCENE TRANSITION*]

Entering through the front door, Jeff heads toward the office (the room that Larry is in). Richard heads in the opposite direction. Richard enters the kitchen, sees the half-eaten piece of cake and picks up the plate (*looking around/in the direction of Jeff*). Susie enters the kitchen, see's Richard holding the cake and verbally assaults him for being a hypocrite.

Susie: "Richard! You lying, diet-cheating, FANCY PANTS, afro-headed ASSHOLE."

Jeff enters the kitchen without Larry. Richard demands Jeff confess to eating the cake. Jeff denies eating the cake. Jeff says he wasn't even in the kitchen and points out that Richard is the one holding the cake. (*The dog continues to make belching noises (audio dub)—drawing stares from all*). Susie turns to Richard.

Susie: "Richard...take your gasbag, saggy balled dog and get THE FUCK OUT."

Richard picks up the dog and stomps off in a huff.

Jeff (yelling after Richard): "And take your salami with you."

Jeff tells Susie he is impressed she defended him and is really 'turned on' by it. Jeff asks her if she wants a 'quickie'. Susie smiles at Jeff.

Susie: "You'll always be MY FAT FUCK. Now, come over here (*gestures to Jeff*), big boy, and get a piece of what you've been wanting all week…"

(*Camera angle from behind Jeff*) Jeff looks at Susie and then at the chocolate cake (*positioned between them*). (*The camera shot switches back and forth between Susie and the chocolate cake*).

FADE OUT/Cue Music.

(END)

Where ARE You? *Standing Around...*

One of our favorite ironies of tolerating the World's WORST Boss was his regular use of several demeaning phrases meant to motivate and/or inspire us to work harder. They did...just not in the way he intended.

The World's WORST Boss was a control freak... harmlessly, at first. We would receive endless amounts of email demanding we follow his exact instructions. When wasn't sending us childish email, he was calling us, demanding we check in with him before AND after all project meetings. We found his behavior amusing and unprofessional, so we intentionally ignored it. One evening, after arriving at work 5 minutes later than anticipated, we received the following harassing email: "When I say I want you at the location at 11:15pm, I MEAN 11:15, not 11:16, not 11:20, 11:15!...Is THAT understood?????"

The resulting discussion:
Ray: "What school grade are we in, again?"

John: "Take some notes, we're going to get a sitcom scene out of this......"

And we did, and more. In terms of control freaks, this next behavior has to be the gold standard. The World's WORST Boss began sending us cell-phone text messages and PC – Instant Messenger notes. They were always the same simple message:

"WHERE ARE YOU?"

[77]

On the surface, it was demeaning and childish. Demanding "WHERE ARE YOU?" of 40-something year olds was unprofessional and pointless….but the truly, TRULY motivating aspect to this: at various times he would send these when we were sitting within six feet of him. We would stand up and look over a divider, or turn around in our chairs and ask him: "Do you require some assistance?" When we managed to stop laughing, we scribbled down notes, which found their way into our lead episode, 'My SPACE'.

Of course, it didn't end there. In assessing our on-the-job performance in LA, the World's WORST Boss would repeatedly comment to us: "There's a lot of standing around going on here." Standing around—meaning, we weren't working on something with the greatest of intensity for every waking moment. Apparently, he thought the insult was some sort of motivational tool. And again, it was. In fact, by logical extension, we considered HIM a motivational TOOL. And we did work 'harder'...only not on anything relevant to him. Each time that idiotic phrase came out of his mouth, it sent us to another room to work harder...on our sitcom material. It got to the point where it was so 'inspirational', that in order not to laugh in his face, we had to sprint out of the room whenever he said it.

…..Of course, even Mother Teresa was known to occasionally tell a pushy dimwit, *FUCK YOU!**

---

*Blatant LIE. Mother Teresa <u>never</u> said that……she used the polite variation, *Cluck*...

Episode 5

"Cluck YOU!"

Synopsis: Larry suspects his girlfriend of cheating on him and assumes a secret identity to prove it while Leon acquires a powerful floral scent that puts a kink in his game.

Scenes: 15

Cast: Larry, Jeff, Leon, Richard, Antoinette, Larry's Girlfriend, Un-named male friend, Homeless man.

Special Guest: ChickenGuy - man in chicken costume – Ron Palillo* or Gilbert Gottfried.

* Ron Palillo, best known for his role as Arnold Horshack on the 1970s television comedy "Welcome Back, Kotter," was our first choice for the role when we wrote the episode in early 2012. Ron tragically passed away in August of 2012. R.I.P., Ron.

"Cluck YOU!"

1. INT. LARRY'S HOUSE – DAY-NIGHT (ONE)

Larry is sitting on the couch. Leon enters the room. Larry is holding a five dollar bill and tells Leon he needs change and asks Leon if he can break the five. Leon asks Larry why he needs to break the five. Larry tells Leon it's for tipping purposes. Leon says he can break the five. He leaves the room to get the change. Leon returns...takes the five from Larry's hand and puts 20 quarters (loose) in Larry's hand.

Larry: "What is this?"

Leon: "It's your tipping money!"

Larry: "I was thinking more like dollar bills!"

Leon: "You going to a tittie bar or something 'cuz you gonna need more than that!"

Larry looks into his hand filled with quarters.

Larry: "Never mind."

Larry reminds Leon he needs to leave the house. Larry has prepared a special dinner for his girlfriend and she will be arriving soon. Leon agrees and leaves the house. Larry checks the time on his wristwatch (*close-up on his watch--approximately 7pm*). Larry picks up the cell phone and calls his girlfriend. The call goes directly into voicemail. Larry hangs up. Larry checks the time on his wristwatch (*close-up on his watch--approximately 7:15pm*). Larry picks up the cell phone and redials his girlfriend. The call goes directly into voicemail. (*The camera zooms out to view the dining room table.*) Larry has set up a romantic dinner with a white tablecloth, crystal wine glasses, and lit candles. Larry (*tapping on the table*) continues waiting for his girlfriend to arrive for the special romantic dinner. The camera zooms in to the clock on the wall (*the hands on the clock advance fast forward two hours*). The camera returns to a shot of the dining room. The candles have burned themselves out and Larry is asleep on the couch (*an empty wine glass slipping from his hand*).

Larry's girlfriend enters the house. Larry awakens and questions her of her whereabouts and why she was late for dinner. The girlfriend tells Larry there was lots of traffic. Larry asks about her cell phone and why it went straight into voicemail. The girlfriend says the battery died. Larry does the 'LIE stare' and acknowledges her with an 'OK.' The girlfriend walks away from Larry. Larry (*camera close-up on the back of the girlfriend*) notices the back of her hair is messed up, flattened and the back of her shirt is wrinkled/pulled out. Larry stares, opens his mouth, but says nothing. The girlfriend says she's tired and is going to sleep. Larry asks about the dinner he prepared. The girlfriend replies: 'Freeze it.' Larry (suspicious, frustrated, irritated) mumbles to himself.

2. INT. RESTAURANT - DAY (TWO)

Larry is seated at a table having lunch with Jeff and Richard Lewis. Richard and Jeff are asking Larry about his hot girlfriend. Larry tells the story of her being late for dinner and suspects her of cheating on him and being a player. Jeff asks Larry if he smelled cologne on her or if he noticed any beard rash.

Larry: "Beard rash?"

Jeff: "Beard rash, Larry. You know ---her face or neck or...ahhhh, other parts, have red streaks where some guy was rubbing his face."

Richard Lewis: "There are always signs but you have to look for them."

Larry says he didn't notice anything. Larry says he tried to call his girlfriend and the calls went right into voicemail. She said her phone battery died. Larry recalls/tells Richard and Jeff how he noticed her hair was messed up and flat in the back as if she was on her back plus the back of her shirt was wrinkled and pulled out. Richard says maybe she was wrinkled and pressed from the car...the headrest could flatten her hair and the car seat could wrinkle her shirt.

Jeff: "What else you got?"

Larry: "She immediately went up the stairs as if she was avoiding me."

Richard Lewis: "Maybe she wanted you to follow her...you know...for sex."

Larry: "She said she was tired and was going to sleep."

Jeff: "You need to keep an eye on her to get to the bottom of this. Maybe you should hire a private investigator. The last thing you need are sloppy seconds!"

Richard agrees.

Jeff: "You, my friend, want to go where no man has gone before!"

Larry: "Ok, Captain Kirk...at our age, everyone has gone there before."

Larry looks at his watch and says he needs to leave to pick up his car from the detail shop down the street. Larry puts down cash for his lunch but Jeff says he'll take care of it. Jeff asks if he needs a ride but Larry refuses and says he will walk. Larry stands and leaves.

3. EXT. PUBLIC STREET/SIDEWALK - DAY (TWO)
Larry is walking down the street towards the detail shop. Larry approaches a person dressed in a chicken costume. The chicken character is actively moving around, dancing and handing out coupons. Larry cautiously approaches the ChickenGuy. ChickenGuy offers Larry coupons for a free appetizer, shake or soft drink. Larry refuses the coupon and gets in a debate over not taking the coupon. Larry asks the ChickenGuy about the costume and his job. Larry tells him he has always been interested in doing a costume role -- dressing up in a character outfit ('not a chicken...more like Mickey Mouse or Goofy'). ChickenGuy talks about all the hot 'chicks' that dig the costume and approach him for hugs and pictures.

ChickenGuy: "Mickey and Goofy can't get grown-up ass. Sometimes I can cop an 'accidental' feel, ya know what I mean? ChickenGuy loves his job and everyone loves the ChickenGuy."

ChickenGuy asks Larry the time...Larry looks at his watch and says it's 12:05. ChickenGuy says he would like to continue talking with Larry, but he's 5 minutes past his lunchtime and he has to take a break. ChickenGuy tells Larry that if he can come back tomorrow before noon,

Larry can be ChickenGuy during his lunch break. Larry agrees. ChickenGuy repeats to Larry that he needs to be there before noon or the deal is off.

ChickenGuy: "Noon! Not 12:01, not 12:02, not 12:05, NOON!"

Larry agrees. Larry continues walking towards the detail shop.

4. EXT. CAR DETAIL SHOP - DAY (TWO)
Larry is standing at the garage entrance of an auto detailing shop looking for his car. A car attendant with a heavy foreign accent approaches.

Car Attendant: "Good afternoons, Mr. DA-Vid! Your car will be right out."

Larry's Prius pulls around the corner and stops next to Larry. Larry walks around the Prius observing and admiring the detail job and comments how it looks brand new. The car attendant opens the door to let Larry see the inside of the car. Larry sits in the driver's seat and immediately gets a whiff (sniffing) of a strong scent of air freshener.

Larry (choked up): "What is that?....is that jasmine?"

Larry complains that he specifically requested NO air freshener. The attendant apologizes but says it's too late...there's nothing they can do. Larry notices the loose change in his center compartment is gone. Larry complains to the attendant. The attendant says the change must have been lost when the car was vacuumed. The attendant points to a sign on the side of the shop that states 'Not responsible for missing items, change, antennas, etc.' Larry looks at the sign and points out another sign that says 'Tips appreciated'.

Car Attendant (with a heavy accent): "You like to leave tip?"

Larry: "Your tip's in the vacuum!"

Larry coughs, frowns, lowers driver's side window and drives away.

5. EXT. LARRY DRIVING HIS PRIUS ON THE STREET - DAY (TWO)

Larry stops at a traffic light and is startled by a knocking on his passenger side window. Larry looks at a homeless man shaking a cup asking for loose change. Larry motions and says, 'not interested.' The homeless man continues to knock on the window. Larry finally opens the passenger window to tell him he doesn't have any change. The homeless guy puts his head into the window...(*sniffs*) gets a whiff of the overly strong air freshener scent and begins to cough and choke. The homeless man, choking, coughing and backing up (shouts), 'Is that jasmine? Your car smells like a whorehouse!' Larry drives away.

6. INT. LARRY'S OFFICE - DAY (TWO)

Larry is entering the office and stops to talk with Antoinette. Antoinette (*sniffs*) comments about the scent coming from Larry.

Antoinette: "What's that scent, Larry?...were you just with a woman?"

Larry replies, 'No.' Antoinette doesn't believe it and continues to question Larry. Larry asks Antoinette for her advice on finding out if a woman is cheating...'What are the signs?' Antoinette asks Larry if he is cheating on his girlfriend and trying not to get caught. Larry explains that he suspects his girlfriend. Antoinette suggests Larry openly talk with his girlfriend and see what she has to say.

Antoinette: "Open and honest communication is always best."

Larry: "Not in this case...I can't even get a goodnight kiss out of her let alone a conversation!"

Larry walks away from Antoinette to his office. (*Camera close-up on the back of Larry.*) Antoinette observes the back of Larry's shirt is wrinkled.

Antoinette: "You WERE with a woman Larry...your shirt back is completely wrinkled and un-tucked!"

Larry: "Probably the car seat."

Larry pauses for a few seconds to think about Antoinette's wrinkled shirt observation, and proceeds into his office.

7. INT. LARRY'S HOUSE - DAY (TWO)
Larry is sitting in his living room holding his phone. Larry calls his girlfriend's cell phone. The call goes directly to voice mail. Larry expresses frustration with the call going to voicemail and hangs up. Larry's phone rings.

Larry (out loud): "I bet that's her calling."

Larry answers (*without looking*). Richard Lewis is on the phone asking Larry about his girlfriend and if he's found any evidence she's cheating on him. Richard tells Larry he needs to get to the bottom of this or it will eat at him. Richard suggests checking her for unusual scents – 'like a man's cologne', and Larry follow her when she goes out. Larry tells Richard he is losing his patience waiting for her to come home. Larry sees headlights pan across the room and says to Richard, 'She's here, gotta run!' Larry ends the call. Larry runs to a chair, sits, and pretends to be reading. The girlfriend walks into the house. Larry rises and approaches her. Larry sniffs the air repeatedly to see if he smells men's cologne on her. The girlfriend stops as Larry gets closer. Larry is trying hard (sniffing) to pick up any scent. The girlfriend (sniffing) gets a whiff of Larry and asks who the hell he was with.

Girlfriend: "You smell like whorehouse!...is that jasmine perfume?"

The girlfriend turns and walks towards the stairs. 'I catch you cheating on me, it's OVER!' The girlfriend heads up the stairs.

Larry: "Sex???"

8. EXT. PUBLIC STREET/SIDEWALK - DAY (THREE)
Larry is on a sidewalk dressed in the chicken costume as the ChickenGuy. Larry is making funny movements and noises. ChickenGuy-Larry is getting attention from women and hugs from children. Larry looks up the sidewalk and sees his girlfriend (*acting giddy*) coming out of a storefront/restaurant holding hands with a man. The

girlfriend and the other man walk towards ChickenGuy-Larry.

Larry (angrily talking out loud to himself): "She IS cheating. I'll use the chicken costume and get to the bottom of this."

The girlfriend and the other man approach ChickenGuy-Larry. The girlfriend comments on how adorable and cute the chicken outfit is and how much she loves costumes. The other man steps to the side to take a cell phone call. The girlfriend talks to ChickenGuy-Larry. Larry responds with, 'Cluck-Cluck.' The girlfriend says she really is attracted to the costume and gives ChickenGuy-Larry a long hug. The girlfriend hands ChickenGuy-Larry her business card and whispers in the 'ear' of the Chicken costume that her fantasy is to make love to a character in costume...and how much she has a taste for chicken. The girlfriend tells ChickenGuy-Larry to give her a call sometime. The girlfriend grabs ChickenGuy-Larry's ass through the costume and says quietly..."Call me!" and walks away.

Larry (under his breath): "Cluck YOU!"

Girlfriend (approaches the other man): "Come on baby...let's go!"

ChickenGuy-Larry is furious, and attempts to give her 'the finger'. The chicken costume only has 3 large thick fingers as gloves and ChickenGuy-Larry can't raise the middle finger. Larry's girlfriend sees this but thinks ChickenGuy-Larry is waiving goodbye and returns the wave and winks.

9. EXT. VALET PARKING STAND AT RESTAURANT - DAY (FOUR)

The parking valet opens the car door for Larry. Larry takes the ticket and the valet gets in Larry's car and gags/coughs (from the strong jasmine scent). The valet lowers all the windows and drives away with his head out the driver's side window. Larry enters the restaurant and joins Jeff and Richard at a table for lunch. Richard makes a comment about the strong perfume stink coming from Larry and questions if he was with another woman or a prostitute. Larry explains that the detail shop attendant spread the air freshener inside his car 'like he was having an epileptic seizure.' Larry's cell phone rings. It's the ChickenGuy calling to ask Larry if he would be willing to do another chicken appearance. Larry agrees. Larry explains the chicken costume stand-in work to Jeff and Richard. Larry tells them he caught his girlfriend holding hands with another man but couldn't do anything as he was 'undercover' in the chicken costume. Larry tells them his girlfriend was hitting on him while he was dressed in the ChickenGuy costume and she gave him her card, grabbed his ass, and told him she has some sort of costume sex fantasy. Larry says she had no idea it was him and all he could say was 'Cluck-Cluck.'

Jeff: "You said 'Cluck-Cluck'?"

Larry: "When she was leaving I said, Cluck-YOU."

Jeff: "You said Cluck-YOU?"

Larry: "Yeah!...Cluck-YOU!"

Richard tells Larry that he should 'go for it.'

Richard: "Since you're not getting any pussy as Larry, you might as well get it as the Chicken Bone."

Larry: "Chicken-GUY, you schmuck."

Larry (*turns his head*) thinks about Richard's comment.

10. INT. LARRY HOUSE - NIGHT (FOUR)
Leon approaches Larry and asks for the keys to the Prius. Larry questions Leon as if he were a teenager wanting to borrow the car. Leon says he has a date but will be back early because he has a second date later that same night. Leon grabs the keys and says: 'Thanks Dad!', and leaves the house. 30 seconds later, Leon returns coughing and choking.

Leon: "WHAT THE FUCK is that smell in your car?...I can't drive it smelling like that!...the Prius smells like…like a pussy!...C'mon LD, it's already hard enough for any man trying to get pussy driving a Prius!"

Larry pauses to think about the lack of Prius pussy.

Larry: "You're saying the Prius ISN'T a pussy magnet?"

Leon (extending his hand towards Larry): "Gimmee cab fare."

Larry hands him some cash and Leon hurries out of the house still coughing and choking. Larry's cell phone rings. The ChickenGuy is calling Larry and asks for a favor. The ChickenGuy asks Larry if he can pick-up the chicken costume tonight and stand-in as the ChickenGuy tomorrow (Friday) because he needs to go to court for a lawsuit against a former employer. Larry agrees. The ChickenGuy tells Larry to meet him outside the restaurant in 20 minutes and he'll give Larry the chicken costume. Larry agrees.

ChickenGuy: "Don't be late. Twenty minutes, Larry. Not twenty-one, not twenty-two, twenty minutes."

11. EXT. PARKING LOT IN FRONT OF RESTAURANT - NIGHT (FOUR)

Larry is driving in his Prius. He pulls into a parking spot in front of the restaurant, parks and waits. A knocking on the passenger window startles Larry. The ChickenGuy (*holding the costume*) gestures and Larry lowers the passenger window. The ChickenGuy breaths in/notices a strong scent of jasmine air freshener and begins to choke/gasp. The ChickenGuy asks Larry if he's wearing ladies perfume. Larry tries to explain. The ChickenGuy is in a rush (backing up and gasping). The ChickenGuy tosses the chicken costume through the passenger side window. The ChickenGuy thanks Larry for the favor and says he will call him over the weekend to arrange a pickup of the chicken costume. Larry agrees, picks up the chicken costume...looks at it, smiles, and tosses it in the back seat.

12. EXT. LARRY'S DRIVEWAY - NIGHT (FOUR)

Larry pulls into his driveway, gets out of the car, closes the door and locks the car with the remote (*audio dub: 'chirp'*). Larry walks towards the house. (*Camera shot shows the chicken costume in backseat of car*).

13. INT. LARRY'S HOUSE - NIGHT (FOUR)

Larry enters his home and sees Leon lying on the couch looking distressed. Larry walks over to Leon. Larry questions Leon why he's back so soon from his date. Leon says his date got a whiff of the pussy Prius scent on his shirt and accused him of cheating.

Leon: "No date. No pussy."

Leon gets a whiff of Larry and moves away from him. Leon stands, says he's going to take a shower to scrub the stink off him, then burn the clothes he wore before his next date is ruined too.

Leon (walking away) shouts: "The house of no pussy, Larry!"

Larry brings his shirt sleeve to his nose trying to smell what everyone's talking about but can't smell anything.

Larry (shouting): "Did my girlfriend call?"

Leon (shouting, off camera): "No pussy, Larry."

14. EXT. PUBLIC STREET/SIDEWALK - DAY (FIVE)
Larry is standing on the sidewalk dressed as ChickenGuy, handing out coupons. He greets people and attempts a few 'dance moves'. Leon is passing by, approaches and sees ChickenGuy-Larry dancing (*like a 'clumsy white guy'*). Leon gets close, sniffs, and gasps from the jasmine smell.

Leon: "LD? Dat you? What the fuck are you doing? You look like Frosty the Snow-chicken having a seizure! You got them moves all wrong!"

Larry: "Oh!...WHAT do you know, mister? I have all the moves."

Leon: "I'd tear that shit up and show you moves like that 'Circus So-laid' shit!"

Larry and Leon banter until Larry agrees to let Leon wear the chicken costume to show off his moves. Larry says he needed a break anyway and could use a cup of coffee. Leon, (still gasping) says there's a coffee shop across the street.

15. INT. COFFEE SHOP - DAY (FIVE)

Larry is sitting by a window inside the coffee shop drinking coffee. He looks across the street at Leon in the chicken costume. Leon is moving and dancing around with 'funky' chicken moves and getting lots of attention from people walking by and cars driving past. Larry, (from inside the coffee shop) sees his girlfriend approaching ChickenGuy-Leon. Leon and Larry's girlfriend are dancing together on sidewalk, grinding/touching in a sexual manner. Larry sees his girlfriend lean in and appear to say something into ChickenGuy-Leon's ear. ChickenGuy-Leon tosses the coupons onto the curb and walks off with Larry's girlfriend (*Leon's hand on her ass*).

16. INT. LARRY'S HOUSE - DAY (FIVE)

Larry is talking on his phone. He tells Jeff that he saw his girlfriend walk off with Leon. Larry's hears a car pull up (*audio dub*) and presumes it's his girlfriend approaching the house and ends the call. The girlfriend enters the house and walks toward Larry. Larry greets her. The girlfriend stops in front of Larry. Larry notices a yellow feather on her shirt.

Larry: "You have something on your shoulder (leans in, sniffs)...Have you been around some chickens?"

Girlfriend: "I guess I did have some chicken..."

Larry: "What kind of chicken?"

Girlfriend: "What do you mean?...What kind of chicken?"

Larry: "White meat?...dark meat?"

Girlfriend: "Dark meat..."

Larry: "Reaaaalllly?"

Girlfriend (annoyed): "Why does it matter?"

Larry sniffs again (*moving in close to the girlfriend*)

Larry: "I know this smell from somewhere!"

Girlfriend: "You know what, Larry?...I don't need this shit anymore! (*The girlfriend turns and proceeds up the stairs.*) I'm getting my stuff and leaving...Fuck You, Larry."

Larry: "Fuck me?.....CLUCK YOU!"

Leon enters house and greets Larry.

Larry: "...AND what have you been up to all afternoon?"

Leon walks past. (*Camera close-up on the back of Leon.*) Larry turns and observes the back of Leon's shirt is wrinkled and pulled out.

Leon: "Not much...just Cluckin' around!"

FADE OUT/Cue Music.

(END)

- 11 -
Reaching Out – First Contact

Ray said it would be easy --"We just get our stuff together and give it to a big shot like Larry David." John, always the skeptic, would invariably ask: "How? Where? How do you 'give it' to a big shot, like Larry David?" Ray always had the answer…."Don't you worry about that, tough guy." Larry David, however, would be about as easily reached as any current Sports Illustrated swimsuit cover model. (Note to self—look into trading a pony for a swimsuit model.)

It may be cliché, but it's true. Southern California has its share of fakes and phonies aspiring to be in the TV and film industry. Everywhere we looked, everyone we met 'knew' an industry big shot that could connect us with Larry David or HBO. A couple of introductions at a party alleged they knew the writers of the South Park series and could introduce us to them. Every other bartender and waiter/waitress had 'SURE FIRE' advice for getting our scripts into the hands of producers that worked at HBO. A casual acquaintance had a cousin who was a writer at Disney and could make introductions for us. All dead ends.

That didn't stop us from looking. It didn't take long for us to figure out that there was virtually no contact info for Larry David to be found anywhere. Larry is something of a non-technology user. He doesn't use social media. If he even has email, it's a well-guarded address. And a phone number is simply out of the question. So we looked at our options. Larry's agent or manager? Larry, at some point (and we can only assume, as it's rarely referenced) signed with and is represented by the biggest agent at the most respected talent agency in Hollywood: Ari Emanuel at WME (or William Morris Endeavor). Mr. Emanuel would NOT be taking our calls or emails. Not a problem, we resolved ("Don't you worry about that, tough guy"). There were plenty of other associated individuals. We tracked down contact information and reached out to Curb Your Enthusiasm Executive Producers, Tim Gibbons, Alec Berg, and Director Robert Weide, as well as some other lesser-associated Curb and HBO individuals.

We also reached out to established TV and film people that we located on Facebook, Twitter, LinkedIn and even their own personal web pages—Gabe Kaplan, Albert Brooks, Paul Rieser, even Jerry Seinfeld. The response was consistent...in that there was never a response.

For the moment, we were stunned and discouraged...down, but NOT out, as *Time Heals*......

- 12 -

Episode 6

"Time Heals NO Wounds"

Synopsis: Larry acquires a super-hero power and uses it at his high school reunion to make amends to an old girlfriend but his new-found power isn't enough to keep him from repeating a humiliating occurrence that caused her to have a mental meltdown.

Scenes: 13

Cast: Larry, Leon, Richard Lewis, Jeff, Restaurant Gossiping Women + Customers in restaurant, Prom Date, Pool-side Women, High School Classmates, Golf Course Workers and Crowd, Infomercial Announcer (voice only).

Special Guest: Our short list became too short. We originally thought of using Davy Jones and Mike Nesmith (of The Monkees) as the dueling sports-comics store clerks. With Davy Jones unfortunate passing, we considered the following actors for the role of the male sports-comics store clerk: Michael Clarke Duncan and Larry Hagman. We presume including them on our short list didn't put them on God's short list (both passed away in 2012)...so we're making this the *Reader Participation section*. Read the episode and suggest a (living!) actor for the role. Send your suggestions to:

BigCarlProductions@gmail.com

"Time Heals NO Wounds"

1. INT. LUNCH AT RESTAURANT – DAY (ONE)

Larry is having lunch/coffee with Richard Lewis at a diner type restaurant. Larry is speaking with Richard and notices from across the room, two women that keep turning their heads, looking at Larry, then talking and laughing to themselves. (*Repeats several times.*) Larry is distracted/curious as to why they are glancing at him and laughing. Richard jokingly tells Larry he should walk over to their table and get to the bottom of it. The two women look at Larry one more time, laugh and turn away. Larry is annoyed but curious, stands up and heads towards their table. Richard pleads with Larry to come back and sit down.

Richard: "What are you, nuts? People get murdered every day doing that sort of thing."

Larry walks up to the women.

Larry: "Excuse me, I couldn't help noticing that little 'women thing' you were doing."

Woman to Larry: "Women thing?"

Larry: "You know, the 'Twist 'n Babble'."

Woman to Larry: "Sir, I don't know who you think you are but you should mind your own fucking business!" (*The two women look at each other, holding in their laughs.*)

Larry: "So you weren't talking about me or my friend?"

Larry looks in the woman's eyes (does the 'LIE *stare*') and says 'Ok.' Larry returns to the table with Richard Lewis.

Richard asks what happened. Larry says it was the 'Twist 'n Babble' thing that all women do.

Larry (to Richard): "Guys never do the 'Twist 'n Babble'."

Richard: "You know what Larry? Men don't give a shit like woman do…they say what they have to say and that's it. Women would keep talking even if their heads exploded."

Larry: "I'd still like to know what those two were talking about."

Richard: "You know you'll never find out…that's a woman's code. Those secrets are locked up tighter than a nun's ass."

Larry (giving Richard a puzzled look): "A nun's ass?"

Larry and Richard finish lunch and get up to leave the restaurant. As they pass by the two women, Larry looks at the woman who just told him off and she deliberately fakes a whisper to her friend and makes (*audible/audio dub*) 'Pssst…Pssst…Pssst' whisper noises to annoy Larry.

2. INT. LARRY'S HOUSE – NIGHT (ONE)
Larry and Leon are sitting on the couch watching television. Larry asks Leon if he's ever had women talk about him, 'you know…gossip', while they were in the same room.

Leon: "Bitches talk about the BIG L all the time."

Larry asks Leon if that bothers him.

Leon: "Nope. Not at all. They all want a piece of this (*grabs his crotch*), so what do I give a fuck what they talk about!"

Larry looks down at his own crotch.

Larry: "Look, I don't think they want a piece of this but I wish I knew what they were saying."

Leon tells Larry to quit acting like a pussy...all nosey and shit! Leon announces he's going to bed and heads up the stairs. Larry flips through channels on the TV and sees an infomercial for the 'EXTREME-Ear'. The infomercial announcer promises the device can pick up whispers 'up to a thousand feet away! It's the perfect eavesdropping device.' Larry picks up the phone, dials, and orders one.

3. INT. JEFF'S OFFICE – DAY (TWO)

Larry is sitting in Jeff's office. Larry tells/describes to Jeff the Extreme-Ear device he ordered and is expecting it to arrive today or tomorrow. He's waiting for a call from Antoinette to let him know when the package arrives. Larry tells Jeff about his 40-year high school class reunion. Larry says he's not sure if he wants to go. Larry tells Jeff about a time capsule they buried 40 years ago at the senior graduation and that it will be re-opened at the 40th reunion. Larry tells Jeff that he was at the original placement ceremony for the capsule and was asked to contribute something and that he searched through his pockets and told the teacher, 'All I have is this baseball card.' He didn't think they would want it, but they said 'yes' so he threw it in to the collection of items to be placed in the capsule. Larry tells Jeff it was an old baseball card he had been carrying in his pocket for weeks. Larry wonders (*out loud*) if it's worth anything today. Jeff asks Larry if he's going to the 'Hole in One' charity challenge at the golf course tomorrow. Larry confirms he will and states this will be his year to get the 'Hole-in-One Grand Prize'...the new Prius! Jeff reminds Larry that he was approached for a project to have Larry host a talk show. Larry makes disparaging remarks about how talk shows are overdone and a great way to kill your career. Jeff suggests Larry think about it. Larry laughs about the idea of being a talk show host but agrees to think about it.

Jeff: "Hey...we've got to try that new Thai fusion restaurant on 3rd Street that just opened up."

Larry questions the word 'fusion' and agrees they should try it.

4. INT. LARRY'S OFFICE – DAY (THREE)
Larry comes out of his office and asks Antoinette if a package has arrived. Antoinette looks through a pile of mail and finds a bubble-wrapped package and hands it to Larry. Larry looks at the return label (EXTREME-Ear, INC.), smiles and takes it back to his office. Larry is at his desk unpacking the box and reading the poorly translated instructions (*aloud*).

Larry: "Best you charge Extreme-Ear at least 60 minute before using to get you the maximum effective range and life batter."

Larry: "Life batter?"

Larry sighs and continues reading.

Larry: "The static noisy may be heard when batteries have power not more than 10% remaining power."
Larry sighs and nods.

Larry: "Static noisy?"

Larry's office phone rings. It's Jeff calling and Larry answers. Jeff tells Larry the 'Hole in One' event at the golf course is starting in an hour and wants to know where Larry is.

Larry (looking at his Extreme-Ear) says he's running late but will get there as fast as he can. Jeff reminds Larry that he might not have enough time to hit some practice balls. Larry says he'll be fine and ends the conversation. (*Camera shot of the clock. The clock minute hand ticks forward*). Larry stares at the Extreme-Ear. (*Camera shot of the clock. 30 minutes have passed*). Larry impatiently grabs the Extreme-Ear and leaves his office.

5. EXT. GOLF COURSE – DAY (THREE)
Larry meets up with Jeff at the 'Hole in One' tee watching the others being called by name. Jeff asks Larry if he had time to hit any practice balls. Larry says no. Larry asks Jeff how he did. Jeff says, 'Don't ask.' Jeff looks at the tee-off list and observes Larry is next. The starter calls, 'Larry David…you're up.' Larry walks up to the tee and prepares to swing. Before he swings he touches his ear and realizes he has the Extreme-Ear in his ear. He adjusts it and begins to hear the other players in the background. (*Audio dub*) 'He's aiming right!…He's way right.' Larry adjusts his stance with each overheard comment. The other players get irritated that Larry is taking a long time to hit his ball. As Larry starts to swing, he hears (*audio dub*) 'bald

asshole' and shanks the ball. Larry (*upset*) shouts out to the onlookers/players, 'I heard that!'

Jeff (to Larry): "Heard what?"

Larry: "This is what I was telling you about yesterday, the Extreme-Ear. You can hear people up to a thousand feet away like they were next to you. One of those schmoes in the crowd called me a bald asshole right as I was swinging. I should get a do-over."

Jeff tells Larry he is like an FBI eavesdropper or spy. Larry is excited about how well he can hear and that it's almost like having a superpower. Jeff points out it might be dangerous, like the guy calling Larry an asshole when he was at the golf tee and how it broke his concentration. Larry agrees. [SCENE TRANSITION]

Jeff and Larry are walking/cutting through the golf course pool area on the way to the parking lot. Larry (touches his ear) and picks up a conversation coming from the opposite end of the swimming pool. (*Audio Dub-garbled conversation*). Larry says to Jeff, 'Wait, I hear something!' Larry turns his head scanning the pool area for the source. Larry sees two women tanning by the pool having a conversation. Larry hears one of the women complaining.

Pool-side woman (*audio dub*): "My husband never notices me anymore. He never takes me out, even when I go above and beyond to look good for him. I do my hair and nails, I even went for one of those Brazilian waxes. I wish someone would just notice since I put forth so much effort."

Larry tells Jeff to follow him and to 'pay attention.' Larry and Jeff approach the women. Larry pauses and compliments the complaining woman.

Larry: "Wow, you look incredible! What are you doing here? You are too good looking to belong to this club, especially with those beautifully manicured nails and hair that shines like the sun."

The woman smiles at Larry's compliments.

Larry: "Let me ask you something...Are you married?"

Pool-side woman: "Unfortunately."

Larry: "Ahhh, too bad. I'd love to flaunt you around town."

The woman is (*visibly*) excited to receive the compliment. She gets off her chair, gives Larry a hug and a kiss on the cheek and tells Larry, 'You just made my day.' Larry looks at Jeff and Jeff gestures in amazement by Larry's super-hearing abilities.

[*SCENE TRANSITION*]

Larry and Jeff are leaving the golf course.

Jeff (to Larry): "You, my friend, DO have a superpower. The power of Super-Bullshit."

Larry (*touches his ear*) hears a faint/distant conversation (*audio dub*). Larry turns his head scanning the parking lot for the source. Larry spots two guys talking in the middle of the lot. Larry motions Jeff to stop. (*Audio dub*)

'Hey...there's Larry David...the bald asshole who couldn't hit a straight golf shot if he was in a subway tunnel.' Larry tells Jeff to hold on as he needs to take care of something.

Larry (shouts toward the men): "Nice hair plugs you prick! Did you get them at the dollar store?"

Jeff: "What was that all about?"

Larry (pointing to his ear): "EXTREME-Ear."

Jeff nods and reminds Larry that he made reservations at the Thai fusion restaurant for tomorrow. Jeff assures Larry he will be back before the class reunion starts, if Larry decides to go.

6. EXT. DRIVING IN PRIUS – DAY (THREE)
Larry is driving in his Prius. Richard Lewis calls. Larry answers the phone. Richard tells Larry that the two women that were in the restaurant the other day are back again.. The woman are doing the 'Twist & Babble' to him this time. Richard suggests Larry come to the restaurant right away. Larry touches his ear (EXTREME-Ear) and says he's near the restaurant and will be there in two minutes. Larry makes a quick u-turn.

7. INT. RESTAURANT FROM SCENE 1 – DAY (THREE)
Larry walks into the restaurant and spots Richard sitting in a booth. Larry approaches, greets and joins Richard. Richard gestures to the two women seated across the restaurant. One of the women notices Larry, flips him off and turns toward her girlfriend and makes remarks to her friend while laughing. Larry tells Richard about his new 'super-hero power' (*touches his ear*) and turns on the

Extreme-Ear. Larry repeats what the women are saying to Richard. Richard doesn't believe that Larry is actually hearing both women's detailed discussion and says Larry is making it up. Larry repeats the women's conversation to Richard. 'The women love being gossipy when no one can hear them.' Larry continues (tells Richard), 'the woman on the left – the one who told me to mind my own fucking business is discussing with her girlfriend a recent medical issue of incontinence and loss of bladder control. She says she starts peeing or spotting without any warning and how embarrassing it is and how she can't tell anyone. She insists her girlfriend keep this a secret. Richard tells Larry that they need to leave and he has already paid. Larry and Richard pass by the two women as they leave the restaurant. Larry looks at the woman who continues to mock him. She deliberately fakes a whisper to her friend making 'Pssst…Pssst…Pssst' whisper noise (*audio dub*) loud enough to annoy Larry. Larry pauses at their table.

Larry (loud): "Jennifer!...So good to see you!....How's your incontinence problem going?...Are you still pissing all over the place?....Piss, Piss, Pissst."

The woman cringes with embarrassment as the other customers in the restaurant turn and look. Larry and Richard exit.

8. INT. LARRY'S HOUSE-KITCHEN – DAY (FOUR)
Leon and Larry are sitting at the kitchen table having breakfast. Leon is reading a magazine (Journal of Scientific Medicine).

Leon (to Larry): "Scientific studies show that women use an average 13,000 more words per day than men. Women use up 20,000 words in a day and men use about 7,000."

Leon doubts that he speaks 7000 words a day and asks if 'grunting' counts. Leon says he doesn't even know more than a couple hundred words altogether. Larry tells Leon that when he was with Cheryl, HE did most of the talking and once in a while, an occasional 'grunting' noise. Leon tells Larry that Cheryl wore the pants in their relationship. Larry disputes who wore the pants. Leon quickly glances around the room commenting on the décor and replies.

Leon: "Look all around you, LD!...We're in a 60's-style Sanford and Son dump and she's livin' large in a luxurious crib!"

Larry looks around the house for a moment (not paying attention to Leon's comments).

Larry: "Cheryl always did look good in pants!"

Leon: "Dammmmmn right!" (*makes "mmm mmm mmm" noise.*)

Larry looks at Leon in anger (*offended*) in response to the "mmm" noises. Leon quickly grabs some food off his plate and repeats the "mmm mmm mmm" noise. Larry's cell phone rings. It's Jeff calling him to remind him of their afternoon lunch at the new Thai fusion restaurant. Larry acknowledges and ends the call.

9. INT. RESTAURANT – DAY (FOUR)
Larry and Jeff are sitting at a table in the Thai fusion restaurant. Jeff tells Larry he will love what he ordered...the

'special' Spicy Thai fusion fish. Larry is holding an invitation/ envelope from the high school reunion and tells Jeff he is still undecided about going to the reunion. The waiter approaches with their lunch special...the Spicy Thai Fusion fish plate. Jeff asks Larry for details about the baseball card he put in the time capsule.

Larry: "It was an early Mantle card, 1952 maybe? What could it be worth?"

Jeff's eyes open wide and he becomes 'animated' (*waving his arms*).

Jeff: "MICKEY MANTLE? A 1952 Mickey Mantle is worth over $10,000. You need to get it back!"

Jeff pushes Larry to go to the reunion and somehow retrieve the card. Larry reminisces to Jeff about his high school prom dance.

Larry: "It was the first time a girl offered to blow me."

Larry describes the intense buildup of that moment and how the girl made Larry feel obligated to 'you know...reciprocate', even though he had never done it before.

Jeff: "So? What did you do?"

Larry: "After the dance, we went back to her parents place and we snuck into her bedroom."

Larry describes how nervous he was to perform 'below the equator.' Larry says while going 'south of the border', he was overcome by the strong 'aroma' and then threw up all over her vagina.

Jeff (laughing): "You puked on her vagina?...what did SHE do?...what did YOU do?"

Larry: "She was shocked and traumatized by it...then she became really angry and told me to get the fuck out!...so I did. She wasn't around school for those last three weeks, so I never got to apologize or say anything to her."

Jeff (laughing) returns focus on the Mickey Mantle baseball card and insists Larry go to the reunion and retrieve it. Larry agrees and wants to find out the current value of the card and obtain a 'replacement/swap' card. Jeff suggests they go to a nearby sports and comics collectibles store after lunch. Larry agrees.

10. INT. ENTRANCE TO SPORTS-COMICS STORE – DAY (FOUR)

Larry and Jeff are walking into a sports and comics collectibles store. The store has one long u-shaped counter that is staffed by a petite Asian woman on one side, and a large, burley man on the other. Larry approaches the woman to inquire about the card.

Larry: "Can you tell me the value of a 1952 Mickey Mantle card?"

The Asian woman replies with a muddled, heavy accent (*tries to pronounce 'Mickey Mantle' but comes out as 'Mini MaTo'*). The woman clerk asks Larry a series of questions about the card (condition, brand, number). Larry turns to Jeff after each question and asks him if he understood her.

The man working the other side of the store yells one-word explanations to them each time (CONDITION, BRAND, NUMBER). The woman clerk eventually shows Larry several versions priced at 9 to 12 thousand dollars. Larry asks to purchase a reprint. The woman clerk does not understand. Larry talks louder.

Larry: "Re-PRINT. RE–PRO–DUC-TION."

The woman clerk tells Larry she does not want to reproduce with him. The man working the other side of the store yells at the woman. The man has a severe stutter. He tries to (*stutters*) tell the woman clerk she is an idiot. He tries to (*stutters*) explain to the woman that Larry wants to buy a copy. He tries to (*stutters*) tell her to find a new career. The woman gets offended and starts screaming (accented/unintelligible) insults at the stutterer. Jeff tells Larry to quickly buy the copy and leave.

[*SCENE TRANSITION*]

Larry and Jeff are walking out of the sports and comics collectibles store. (*Audio dub:* Shouting/stuttering clerks can still be heard). Larry is carrying a baseball card.

Larry (looking at Jeff, says with an exaggerated Asian accent): "Wha da fruck wah dat?"

Jeff (with a mocking stutter): "I, I, d, d, don, don't n,n, fffffffuck,fuck,fuck KING know."

11. INT. LARRY'S HOUSE - DAY (FOUR)
Larry enters his house and calls out to Leon but gets no response. Larry hears faint noises coming from upstairs but

isn't sure of what he's hearing. Larry (*touches his ear*) turns on the EXTREME-Ear. (*Audio dub/Larry hears*) Noisy static is heard briefly, then the sound of Leon and a woman having sex. Larry is offended by the audio and turns off the EXTREME-Ear (*touches his ear*). Larry hears his stomach make a loud growl (*audio dub*) and clutches/presses his stomach. Larry looks at his watch, looks at the reunion invitation, and heads upstairs.

12. INT. HIGH SCHOOL GYMNASIUM - DAY-NIGHT (FOUR)

Larry is at the high school reunion and enters the gymnasium (*decorated with banners and memorabilia*). Larry goes to the refreshments table and spots an obnoxious alumnus named Billy Wolodzko. Larry sees Billy's nametag and attempts to avoid him. Billy grabs Larry's arm and doesn't let go of it. Larry removes Billy's hand from his arm. They chat briefly about their past and what they've been up to. Larry can't stand Billy and quickly excuses himself.

Larry: "Sorry, Billy...I can't take this any longer or I'll blow my brains out...You'll have to excuse me as I need to take a degner before they open up the time capsule."

Billy: "a degner?....So, we'll talk later, then?"

Larry walks away. Larry joins the crowd gathering around the time capsule (*in the middle of the gym floor*). The time capsule is opened. Larry approaches the capsule to examine some of the long-ago deposited items. Larry subtly pulls the substitute baseball card from his pocket and makes the switch. Larry holds up the replacement card. Someone in the group remarks what great condition the card is in. Larry's attention is diverted by Billy Wolodzko. Billy approaches Larry, grabs his arm, and points out a woman across the room and asks Larry, 'wasn't she your prom date?' Larry removes Billy's hand from his arm and observes the attractive, well-dressed woman on the other side of the gym talking with several other classmates. Larry (*touches his ear*) turns on the Extreme-Ear and eavesdrops on her conversation. (*Audio dub - static is heard briefly and then conversation*). The attractive woman is telling the story of her long ago prom date with 'Larry David' to her school friends. She tells them what had happened and how it traumatized her for a long time. Only recently, after YEARS of therapy has she been completely uninhibited in letting a man go 'down on her.' Larry and her eyes meet from across the room. They stare at each other for a moment. Larry 'hears' her say to her friends, (*audio dub*) 'Oh shit, it's HIM. It's Larry.' Her friends tell her to be the bigger person and say hello to him. She refuses because Larry never apologized and how the incident affected her life. Larry hears her say (*audio dub*), 'but he is still so attractive after all these years.' Hearing that, Larry approaches her with two glasses of champagne, hands her one glass and apologizes. Larry says he tried to apologize to her back then, but she had already left school. He tells her how awful he felt and how it traumatized him for a long time and how it took him YEARS of therapy before he could go down on a woman, and only in the last few years has completely overcome his fears. Larry continues to apologize and wants to make it up to her and asks her to dance. They have a drink/toast, and Larry dances with her.

13. EXT. HIGH SCHOOL PARKING LOT - DAY-NIGHT (FOUR)

Larry is walking out of the high school, holding the door open for his former prom date. Larry offers to walk the prom date to her car. The prom date tells Larry she had a wonderful time and asks Larry to sit in her car and chat for a bit. Larry agrees and gets in on the passenger side. The prom date tells Larry how, after all these years, he still looks handsome and she is still attracted to him. Larry tells her she looks sexy and alluring. Larry and the prom date start kissing. While kissing, Larry's stomach makes a loud (*audio dub*) grumbling noise. Larry ignores it and continues kissing.

Prom date: "What was that...that noise?"

Larry apologizes.

Larry: "Sorry, it's nothing—I had a late lunch."

(*Audio dub*) Larry hears Jeff's voice telling him how great the Spicy Fusion fish is, 'order it, you'll LOVE it.'

Larry continues kissing the prom date. The prom date turns her head and sneezes. Larry says 'Gesundheit' to her and she asks Larry for a handkerchief. Larry searches his pockets.

Larry: "I got nothing...all I have is this baseball card" (and shows her the card).

The prom date takes the card from Larry, looks at it for a brief moment and drops it in her lap/crotch area as she covers her face and sneezes again. The prom date searches and finds a napkin in the side of the driver's door and turns to retrieve it. When she turns back towards Larry, they bump heads and Larry's eyeglasses fall off. Larry can't see anything without his glasses and tells the prom date to look for them. Larry says they may have fallen on the floor or between her legs. Larry (*touches his ear*) notices his Extreme-Ear fell out and tells her his hearing aid was also knocked out of his ear. While searching, Larry hears (*audio dub*) the Extreme-Ear emitting static noises. The static noise is coming from between the prom dates' legs. Larry tells the prom date he thinks his glasses are in her seat. To avoid crushing his glasses, he insists she raise her butt off the seat so he can retrieve them. The prom date raises her butt off of the seat, raising her crotch up to his face (with baseball card still in place). Larry leans in towards her crotch area (*camera angle is from behind Larry*) directly over the baseball card. Larry's stomach makes a loud (*audio dub*) grumbling noise. Larry loudly pukes in her lap (*audio dub*).

FADE OUT/Cue Music.

(END)

- 13 -

Inspiration – Treasures *from* Trash

We had been cheated. This came as no surprise. From the beginning of the project that sent us to Los Angeles, big, too-good-to-be-true promises were made to us. Promotions, raises, bonuses, other opportunities, and so on were regularly dangled in front of us. As the project wore on, the promises, one by one, ended up in the trash. No promotions. No raises. A smaller bonus became no bonus. A promise of a large party to celebrate the successful completion was dumped and in its place were tickets to a Chicago Bulls basketball game ---more accurately one ticket each. We could go with each other or surrender our one ticket so the other could take a date. Our initial thought was to give the tickets to homeless people. In the end we gave them to the phone support group who received even less recognition than we did, but the entire incident inspired us in the writing of the episode, 'Scriptably Soft'.

There were other enticements that ended up on the trash pile as well. We were told of upgrades we would receive when we attained 'Diamond' status at the hotel we stayed at and rental car upgrades for 'Gold' status if we were repeat customers. 'Diamond' at the hotel meant 2 candy bars and a Coke at the start of a weeklong stay. Top tier status at the rental car agency meant a single step up from an ultra-sub-compact to a compact. Some of the restaurants at which we became regulars gave us gift certificates – the buy-one get-one offer, but only if we spent over $50. Naturally, that was impossible on the cheapskate $40 per day policy that the company allowed us to spend on meals. Forty, in LA dollars, was easily spent on breakfast and lunch. John was quick to assess these so-called gifts, 'total garbage'.

Trash or not, some of the most useless rewards had value in their inspiration to us and had a strong influence in the creation of our outlines. Truthfully, it wasn't all total garbage. Some of the good 'gifts', we inadvertently ruined. There were other unexpected good gifts...some of which the World's WORST Boss unintentionally 'gave' us.

The best of the gifts were the friends we made. Living a weekday life near El Segundo and Manhattan Beach, California made it natural to visit a number of places on a regular basis --- hotels, restaurants, coffee shops, drug stores, etc. These places and the people at them (AJ at the Hilton, Jerry, Lynne, and the team at Rock 'N Fish, the chicken guy at Versailles, to name a few) became part of our lives. As you read through our episodes, occasionally a specific location is noted, or a minor character is given a specific name---these are small tributes to people and places that are the polar opposite of the people that had sent us to Los Angeles in the first place and were trying to make our lives miserable.

One aspect that the World's WORST Boss obsessed over was that we weren't supposed enjoy one moment while deployed in Los Angeles. He repeatedly reminded us, "You are there on business and NOTHING else."

The other teams accepted that nonsense and lived like robotic hermits. They went from their hotel to the work location, possibly to a restaurant, and back to their hotel, five days a week. In LA, we were LIVING. From visiting the Hollywood sign during the day to watching the sunset on the piers in the evening, from touring Universal Studios to writing scripts, we made the absolute most of OUR time. Naturally, that too was an issue. The World's WORST Boss was angered of course, but limited in retaliation as our onsite work was flawless and meeting all the deadlines. Of course, that didn't stop him from issuing unreasonable project-related demands.

The best of the unexpected gifts was unintentionally 'given' to us by the World's WORST Boss (who would eventually try and 'take it back'). When company management revised our project schedule and committed to an impossible completion date, we painstakingly proved that it was unachievable. The World's WORST Boss responded by (grudgingly) assigning a consultant to us. The consultant, in theory, was going to 'bend' the laws of time and space, and speed our project to its impossible-promised deadline. The consultant, 'Uncle Chad', as he would become known to us, did help us immensely and did speed up our project. But 'Uncle Chad' was also a realist and could see that the process could not be sped up significantly by adding staff to the project.

However, we made one small miscalculation. Uncle Chad became our friend. THAT was not a mis-step. What was a mis-step was allowing that to be discovered by the World's WORST Boss. In mid-project, without warning or discussion, Uncle Chad's monthly contract, which had been automatically renewed every month for the previous four months, was left unsigned. Uncle Chad was, and is one of the finest people we know in Los Angeles.* Even after his contract was terminated, he continued to help us from time to time, purely out of friendship. To us, THAT will forever be a *Gift that Keeps On*......

---

* - At the time of publication, Uncle Chad and his wife, Linda were overseas, on a 'mission' to help the people of Haiti.

Episode 7

"The Gifts That Keep on Giving"

Synopsis: Larry's Birthday party takes on a surreal twist as Larry receives a pile of 'As Seen On TV' type gifts, which cause him even greater grief when he dumps them in the trash.

Scenes: 13

Cast: Larry, Jeff, Susie, Leon, Richard Lewis, Cheryl, Wanda Sykes, Wanda's Auntie, Larry's cousin Velada, various Birthday-Party guests, restaurant staff, clothing store clerk and customer, resale store clerk and customer, credit card company clerk (voice only).

Special Guest: Barbara Eden.

"The Gifts That Keep on Giving"

1. INT. LARRY'S OFFICE - DAY (ONE)

Antoinette hands Larry a (printed) invitation card to review. Larry reviews the sample invitation for his birthday party, before he has them printed and mailed out. Larry reads it out loud and asks Jeff (sitting in his office) if it's appropriate to send out the invitations himself for his own party. He shows Jeff the printed invitation. Jeff notices the card includes in BIG block letters: 'NO GIFTS PLEASE' (camera close-up on "NO GIFTS, PLEASE"). Jeff asks Larry about the 'NO GIFTS' line.

Jeff: "Remember what happened with Ben Stiller and the 'NO GIFTS' invitation?"

Larry snatches the card back from Jeff and reads it out loud.

Larry: "NO GIFTS, PLEASE...Antoinette."

Larry asks Antoinette why she included that line. Larry WANTS gifts. Larry hands the card back to Antoinette, tells her to delete the NO GIFTS line and have it printed and mailed out. Larry announces that he and Jeff are leaving for lunch.

2. EXT./INT. STREET+STORE SCENE - DAY (ONE)

Larry and Jeff are on the street in front of a clothing store, preparing to go their separate ways. Jeff thanks Larry for lunch. Larry goes into the clothing store and Jeff leaves. The store clerk has an E-book reader and is reading an e-book. Larry asks about the E-reader. The clerk shows/tells Larry about it and the book she's reading. Larry tells the clerk he just finished that book and it's a well written piece with an excellent finish. The clerk tells Larry she only has a few pages left and hopes to finish it that day. Larry asks for a pair of pants and the clerk shows him the latest offering.

Clerk: "These are Space-age, ultra-light-weight pants…You've probably seen them on TV…they're durable, 100% wrinkle free, and smooth as silk. You won't even realize you're wearing any pants."

Larry: "Pants FREE?"

Larry takes a pair and goes to the fitting room to try on a pair. Larry emerges from the fitting room to look in a mirror. As Larry approaches the mirror, another customer steps backwards into the aisle. Larry reaches out to keep customer from backing into him, touches the customer on the shoulder and gives her a static electricity shock (*audio dub – popping noise*). Larry apologizes and walks to the mirror. The store clerk comes over (*holding the E-book reader*) and asks Larry how he likes the pants.

Larry: "They seem to have a lot of static cling. I think they caused me to 'shock' that other customer with static electricity."

The clerk disputes it and Larry reaches over to touch her on the arm and touches the E-book-reader. A shock/spark occurs (*audio dub – popping noise*) as Larry touches the E-reader. The clerk looks furious. Larry confirms to the clerk that the pants do cause static electricity. The clerk is not paying attention to Larry and attempts to restart/revive her E-reader. The clerk tells Larry he 'killed' her E-reader. Larry is embarrassed, apologizes and blurts out the ending of the book she was reading. The clerk's face turns red.

Larry tells her the pants don't quite feel like he's 'wearing nothing'...but he'll take them, anyway.

3. INT. LARRY'S HOUSE-ENTRY - DAY (TWO)
Inside Larry's house entryway, party guests arrive, wishing Larry a Happy Birthday and handing him a gift/asking 'where do you want us to put this?' (*Some gifts are wrapped, some are not*). Larry remarks to Richard Lewis (*standing next to Larry*) that people are bringing uninvited guests.

Larry: "Can you believe this? My annoying cousin Velada even brought her half-wit son. The invite didn't say 'AND CHILDREN'."

Richard: "Yeah. The worst moochers and morons always seem to be family members."

Larry (irritated): "The last time she brought her half-wit son to my house, he tried to take a degner in my sink."

More guests arrive. One of Larry's invited relatives arrives for the party bringing/introducing several uninvited relatives. Leon approaches Larry. Larry tells Leon that his annoying relatives, ones that he can barely stand, are bringing uninvited relatives. Leon asks Larry if he wants him to give them a beat down and throw them out on the street.

Leon: "No party at my house ever ended without someone pullin' out a gun or knife."

Larry ponders Leon's offer.

[*SCENE TRANSITION*]

INT. LARRY'S HOUSE-KITCHEN
Susie announces it's time for cake and the guests gather in the kitchen around the table (*waiting for the cake to be brought out*). Larry's cousin Velada announces it's also her young son's birthday and tells Larry it would be nice if the boy could 'help' Larry blow out the candles. Larry resists but is shamed into it by Susie. The cake is brought in from the other side of the room and is set on the table as guests sing Happy Birthday. Larry and Velada's son race to the cake, jockeying for position to the candles. The Birthday song finishes and the boy blows visible blobs of spit (*slow motion or zoom-in*) onto the cake.

Susie: "Who wants cake? Look, we can just scrape this section off...its fine, it's all cleaned off."

None of the guests want cake. Jeff distracts the crowd by announcing it's time to open the gifts. The crowd moves quickly to the living room. Susie is still offering pieces of the spit cake on plates.

[*SCENE TRANSITION*]

INT. LARRY'S HOUSE-LIVING ROOM
Larry sits on the living room couch and opens the gifts. The gifts are total junk—many "As-Seen-On-TV" type gifts (Lint Lizard, Chia-head, Topsy-Turvy planter) and some are duplicated. The gifts accumulate in a large pile in the middle of the room, including a particularly gaudy/odd

statue that is mildly pornographic. Larry opens a decorative box that has no card and contains an intriguing gift – a black, hand painted 'Genie' bottle. Larry opens it and makes a remark about expecting a Genie to come out. Larry thanks everyone for their gifts.

[*SCENE TRANSITION*]

INT. LARRY'S HOUSE-ENTRY
Larry is standing at the entryway sending guests home/thanking them for coming. Leon walks up with a large slice of birthday cake. Larry stares at it.

Leon: "Cake is cake, LD. When we were kids, our birthday cakes were cupcakes that were day-old, fished out of a dumpster."

Leon walks to the gift pile. Larry remarks to Jeff that removing the NO GIFTS line from the invitation may not have been the best idea.

Larry: "What the hell is this? (Larry *gestures to the towering pile of gifts*). Crap they got at Christmas or their own birthdays and didn't want, so they re-gift it to me, just to get rid of it?"

Leon returns from gift pile holding an electric soap dispenser.

Leon: "What da fuck is this, LD?"

Larry sees Jeff and Susie out the door, thanking them for coming.

4. INT. LARRY'S HOUSE-KITCHEN - DAY-NIGHT (TWO)

Leon has set up the electric soap dispenser near the kitchen sink. Larry approaches and tries it. It dispenses a small amount of liquid soap.

Larry (enthusiastic): "This thing is fabulous. Have you tried it?"

Larry tries it 3 times, each time receiving a handful of liquid soap. On the 4th try the dispenser makes a grinding noise (*audio dub*), but no soap is dispensed. Larry tries again and soap gushes out (more than a handful).

Larry (irritated): "This thing is a piece of crap. Have you tried it?"

Leon walks up to it (standing next to Larry), places his hands under it and the dispenser makes a grinding noise (*audio dub*), but no soap is dispensed. Larry suggests he try again. Leon tries again. The dispenser makes a grinding noise (*audio dub*) and a load of soap shoots straight out, onto Larry's pants-zipper. Leon shakes his head and walks away.

5. INT. LARRY'S HOUSE-BEDROOM ROOM – DAY-NIGHT (TWO)

Larry is lying in bed. He picks up the 'Genie' bottle gift, holds it up to the light and looks inside/down the neck of the bottle. He turns it upside down to look for a label and remarks, 'some cheap knock-off, probably.' Larry looks around/scans the room as if to see that he's alone, and rubs the bottle like a magic lantern. Nothing happens. Larry frowns, puts the bottle on the bedside table, lays back and closes his eyes and falls asleep.

6. INT. LARRY'S HOUSE-BEDROOM – DAY-NIGHT (TWO)

[DREAM SEQUENCE – Blurred Fade-in]
Larry is in unfamiliar surroundings (a luxurious bedroom). He picks up the 'Genie' bottle and rubs it. A stream of smoke is released from the bottle and Cheryl ('GenieCheryl') appears to come out of the smoke, dressed seductively as a 'Genie'. Larry reminds her that his every wish is her command. GenieCheryl disagrees. Larry tells her he is her Master and commands her to have a quickie with him. GenieCheryl reluctantly agrees and says that she wants Larry's credit card when they are done. As GenieCheryl seductively approaches Larry, Richard Lewis appears in a doorway draped with beaded strings hanging from the doorframe. Richard calls out, 'Larry', and GenieCheryl disappears in a puff of smoke. Larry is livid. Richard tells him to get a real door with a lock instead of 'beads for drapes' if he wants privacy. Larry sends Richard away and rubs the Genie bottle again. A stream of smoke is released from the bottle and Susie ('GenieSusie') appears to come out of the smoke (dressed seductively) as a Genie. She immediately rips Larry for being a sexist pig, etc. Larry commands her to go back into the bottle and send out GenieCheryl. GenieSusie tells him to fuck off, turns as if to leave, hesitates, reaches past Larry and grabs a box of Godiva Chocolates off the table, then vanishes in a puff of smoke. Larry looks at the bottle, hesitates and rubs the bottle again. A stream of smoke is released from the bottle and Jeff appears to come out of the smoke, dressed 'seductively' in a 'Genie' outfit. Larry jerks awake from the dream.
[END DREAM SEQUENCE]

7. EXT. LARRY'S HOUSE-FRONT/STREET/CURB - DAY (THREE)

Larry and Leon are in the garage/alley piling the junk gifts into a trash can. It piles higher than the rim of the can and Larry can't replace the can lid. Larry places the electric soap dispenser on top of the protruding pile.

Larry (to Leon): "Trash pickup is this afternoon. Let's get this useless junk to the curb."

[*SCENE TRANSITION*]

Larry is driving his car down his driveway towards the street. As he reaches the end of the drive, he stops, reaches out the window, and places the Genie bottle on top of the pile of trash/gifts. As Larry prepares to turn into the street, cousin Velada drives by, sees the trashcan with the gifts spilling out the top, and slows down to glare at Larry.

8. INT. LARRY'S OFFICE - DAY (THREE)

Larry is seated at his desk. The phone rings and Larry answers. The caller was at Larry's birthday party. Larry thanks the caller for attending. The party goer is calling Larry to tell him (*unheard*) that he/she is offended that Larry would throw out the 'carefully selected' gift. Larry claims it was a mistake and that Leon must have put it in the can by accident. (Multiple *complaint calls REPEAT in rapid succession*). Larry tells Antoinette he has a SITUATION to take care of and leaves.

9. EXT. LARRY'S HOUSE-FRONT/STREET/CURB - DAY (THREE)

Larry is approaching his house in his car. He sees the back of a blonde woman in a red dress plucking the black Genie bottle off the top of the pile, getting in her car and driving away. Larry is relieved that the can is still there. Larry turns into his drive and parks in the garage. As he comes out of the garage to retrieve the trashcan, the trash collection truck has pulled up and is in the process of emptying his can into the truck. Larry yells frantically, 'Waaaait', and runs towards the trash collector. The trash collector (*wearing headphones*) can't hear Larry. He gets in his truck and drives forward. Larry chases the truck. He approaches the driver (*the driver removes his headphones*) and tells him he made a mistake and needs his trash back. The trash collector refuses. 'It's not your trash anymore. Once it enters the truck, it becomes city property, and you can't touch it.' Larry argues to no success. Larry returns to the trash can and finds one item stuck at the bottom of the can, a 'Snuggie' blanket wrap. He picks up the grimy box and walks towards the house.

10. INT. LARRY'S HOUSE-KITCHEN – DAY-NIGHT (THREE)
Larry places the dirty Snuggie box on the counter. The phone rings. Larry answers. Wanda Sykes screams (*audio dub*) at Larry saying she saw the trash can full of gifts and how could he throw out the statue she gave him. Larry claims it was a mistake and that Leon put it in the can by accident. Larry lies and says he retrieved it and still has the statue. Wanda continues to yell at Larry. Larry apologizes and ends call. Larry calls out, 'Leon…'.

11. INT. LARRY'S - OFFICE - DAY (FOUR)
The phone rings. Larry looks at the Caller ID (Wanda Sykes), sighs, and answers phone. Wanda screams (*audio dub*) at Larry saying she just saw the statue she gave him in the window of a resale shop on Wilshire and knows Larry

dumped it and lied to her. Larry lies and says it can't be—the one she saw must be a copy. Larry says he has it at home on his kitchen table and Wanda can stop by anytime to see it. Wanda says she will be there in an hour. Larry ends phone call and calls out, 'Antoinette...'.

12. EXT. CITY STREET-STORE FRONT – DAY (FOUR)

Larry and Jeff are standing on Wilshire Blvd outside the resale shop, looking through the window for the statue. Jeff spots it and points it out to Larry. They enter the store and Larry waits in line to buy it. Standing in front of Larry, conducting a transaction is the clothing store clerk (from *Scene 2*). The clothing store clerk turns and recognizes Larry.

Clothing store clerk: "Oh...it's YOU."

Larry: "What brings you here?"

Clothing store clerk: "I traded in my E-reader. You remember –it's the one YOU broke. All I could get was this." (*an electric knife–she 'jabs' it in Larry's direction. Larry steps sideways.*)

The clothing store clerk is angry at Larry and notices the soap stain (*Scene 4*) on his new pants and makes a mocking/crude remark about the stain being a result of static electricity. Larry defends himself reminding the clerk she was the one who picked out the static pants...so it's actually her fault her E-reader broke. They continue to argue over fault of the damaged E-reader. Larry sees the E-reader on the counter and asks the clothing store clerk if she's SURE it's broke? Larry touches the E-reader and a shock/spark occurs (*audio dub*). The E-reader lights up and appears to be working. Larry picks it up and shows the clothing store clerk. Larry 'confirms' to the clerk that the pants do cause static electricity. The clothing store clerk is furious and curses at Larry. Larry looks at the E-reader and tells the clothing store clerk the e-book is right where she left off, and begins reading (a*loud*) the ending of the book. The clothing store clerk's face turns red. She covers her ears and storms out of the resale store. Larry turns to the resale store clerk and asks for the statue. The clerk retrieves it and tells Larry the price. The statue is substantially overpriced. Larry complains.

Resale clerk: "This is NOT the Torrance Flea Market. You want that 'As Seen on TV' junk, go there. Take it or leave it."

Larry grudgingly hands a credit card to the clerk to buy the statue. Larry glances down at the E-reader and asks the clerk how much it is. The clerk tells him he can have it for ten dollars. Larry tells her he will take it. Larry turns to Jeff and explains that Wanda is coming over to check that he still has the statue. The clerk returns, puts the credit card on the counter and asks Larry if he wants the E-reader wrapped for safe transport. Larry asks the clerk about the wrapping. The clerk holds up bubble wrap and 'pops' a bubble, catching Larry's attention. The clerk tells Larry it costs extra. Larry turns and touches the bubble wrap and 'pops' a bubble. Larry's credit card is picked up by a 'creepy-looking' shopper in the store who immediately leaves. Larry declines the wrapping and the clerk places the statue and the E-reader in a bag. Larry picks up the bag and receipt. Larry tells Jeff they better leave before the clerk raises the price. Larry and Jeff leave.

13. INT. LARRY'S HOUSE-KITCHEN - DAY (FIVE)

Larry is returning from the resale store holding the statue as he enters the kitchen. Larry removes it from the bag, places the statue and the E-reader on the counter and hides the bag and receipt. The doorbell rings (*audio dub*). Larry goes to the door and opens it. Wanda is standing there with an elderly woman.

Wanda: "Larry, what the fuck kinda pants you got on?"

Larry says he forgot he was even wearing pants.

Wanda: "Larry...is that a cum stain on the zipper? You are one SICK asshole."

Larry: "These are Space-age, ultra-light-weight pants...You've probably seen them on TV...they're durable, 100% wrinkle free, and smooth as silk. Sometimes forget I'm even wearing any pants. That (*pointing to the zipper*) is a soap stain"

Larry invites them in. They walk towards the kitchen. Wanda introduces the woman as her 'Auntie'. Wanda explains she just picked up her Auntie from the doctor's office where she was being checked for the new pacemaker she had put in last week. Larry reaches out to shake her hand and gives her a huge static electricity shock (*audio dub*). The elderly woman gasps, grabs her chest, stumbles backwards, and knocks the statue off the counter. The statue hits the floor and shatters. Auntie is on the floor, motionless.

Wanda (shouting): "WHAT the fuck Larry, you killed my

Auntie, you static-charged MC Hammer, faggoty-pants muthafucka."

[*SCENE TRANSITION*]

[EXT. LARRY'S HOUSE]
Auntie is being loaded into an ambulance. Wanda is getting into her car, looks at the ambulance and looks back at Larry. Larry (*apologizing*) yells from the front steps, 'It was an accident.' Wanda gives Larry THE finger.

[*SCENE TRANSITION*]

[INT. LARRY'S HOUSE-KITCHEN]
Larry returns to the kitchen and stares at the pieces of the statue on the floor. Larry's phone rings and Larry answers. A credit card company agent is calling Larry to ask about some suspicious activity on his card. The agent (*audio dub*) tells Larry someone has purchased dozens of items at a specialty store using Larry's card. Larry checks his wallet and realizes he left his card at the resale store and tells the credit card company agent it is being used fraudulently. Larry asks the agent what was purchased. The credit card company agent tells him it was used for 27 different items from the "As Seen On TV" store. The credit card company asks Larry to confirm that he did not purchase 7 Snuggie blankets. Larry turns and stares at the grimy Snuggie-blanket box sitting on his kitchen counter and lets out a deep sigh. Larry tells her 'no', and ends the call. Larry sees the E-reader on the counter, steps over the broken statue pieces and reaches for it. As he touches it, a shock/spark occurs (*audio dub – popping noise*), the screen flashes twice (*close up camera shot*) and turns black.

FADE to Black. Cue Music (softly).

FADE-IN:

14. INT. UNKNOWN HOUSE
(*Camera angle shot from behind*) A blonde woman in a red dress is sitting in an oversized chair with a small polishing cloth, gently cleaning the black 'Genie' bottle. (*Camera Pans around to the front of the chair*). A smiling blond woman (Special Guest: Barbara Eden) gently rubs the bottle.

FADE OUT/Cue Music [substitute theme from "I Dream Of Jeannie" by Hugo Montenegro].

(END)

- 15 -

Stalking the BIG SHOTS

Again, Ray said it would be easy. "We just get our stuff together and give it to a big shot like Larry David." Ray's usual reply…"Don't you worry about that, tough guy" was losing its luster. Larry David, still a 'ghost' for all intents and purposes, was not to be found. News reports occasionally surfaced of him in New York, or scouting film locations on the east coast, but nothing that would lead us to any meaningful contact.

Ray accepted that and moved on to our next target of opportunity: Jeff Garlin. Ray made that look easy… even encouraging. At the time, Jeff Garlin was regularly hosting a comic chat show at a notable theater in Los Angeles. Ray bought a ticket, saw the show and then approached Jeff afterward. Jeff was polite and friendly, but not all that inviting in terms of accepting our material. Ray was sure it was only a matter of time. Ray tracked Jeff to a restaurant opening at a 4-Star Chicago hotel, and together, we (Ray and John) crashed the party and found our way over to Jeff. Jeff was again unfailingly polite and even encouraging – No, he didn't need any material, and we should find ourselves an agent to shop our scripts.

An agent? How does one 'get' an agent? Books have been written on the subject. The greatest irony still applied. The best agents won't have anything to do with unknowns and unpublished, and yet, without an agent, we were not likely to ever sell our material or get it published. Getting a crappy agent was, of course, terribly easy. We spoke to several that had a bad 'smell' to them, both figuratively or literally.

Not ones to give up, we changed direction. If we could reach Jeff Garlin, we reasoned, we could reach Susie Essman or JB Smoove (Jerry Brooks).

As luck would have it, Susie Essman and Richard Lewis were scheduled to appear at a benefit in Chicago in 2012. Two for the price of one! EASY...except...one small bump in that road: the event was to benefit a charity, and only charitable donors could attend. OK, so we donate, what's the big deal? We can even write it off on our taxes. The big deal: *"A minimum gift of $5,000 to the Jewish United Fund Annual Campaign is required to attend."* Right...let's find JB Smoove.

Finding Jerry Brooks/JB Smoove was a bit of a *Where's Waldo* search. He's everywhere and nowhere. He has a web page, but no contact information. He has Twitter account but posts schizophrenically – a flood of entries for 4 or 5 days in row and then nothing for 4 or 5 months. His standup comedy appearances were rarely advertised and scattered all over the planet. No progress to be had here.

Still, we pressed on with the 'showcase our sample material to a Curb principal' idea. Richard Lewis came to Chicago to do a standup gig and Ray smooth-talked the club hostess into letting the two of us take a couple of pre-reserved seats after the show began. The PLAN was to hang around until after the show and speak to Richard Lewis when he came out to greet the lingering fans. Otherwise, we would ask if he would come out and take a photo with us. What our plan failed to anticipate: He would not come out at all. "Richard doesn't greet his fans or pose for pictures," we were told by his manager.

So there we stood...in an empty bar with no chance of enticing (or bribing) Richard Lewis with our material. Once again, getting close, but missing an opportunity by a *Hair's* width...

- 16 -

Episode 8

"Hairs Looking at You, Kid"

Synopsis: Larry finds himself in several HAIRY situations that eventually leads to a fiery ending at a celebrity barbeque.

Scenes: 14

Cast: Larry, Jeff, Susie, Leon, Feng Shui woman, Wanda Sykes, Hairy-armed woman, daughter of Hairy-armed woman, Cracker Jack delivery man, Celebrity BBQ guests, TV news crew.

Special Guest: Ron Popeil or "Weird Al" Yankovic as the TV Producer.

"Hairs Looking at You, Kid"

1. INT. LARRY'S BEDROOM – DAY (ONE)
Larry is lying in bed, waking up. Larry discovers a thick, long dark hair on his pillow. Larry puts on his glasses and stares at/examines the hair. Larry gets out of bed, goes into the bathroom and notices a small black hair on his soap. He picks up the soap and holds it close to his face to examine.

2. INT. LARRY'S KITCHEN – DAY (ONE)
Larry enters the kitchen holding up the bar of soap and confronts Leon. Leon is sitting at the table, leaning back in the chair, wearing an unbuttoned shirt. Leon is eating a cupcake and crumbs are falling onto his chest. Larry waves the soap and rants about boundaries and cleanliness. Leon nods to acknowledge Larry, picks the crumbs from his chest and eats them.

Leon: "LD...we're all FAMILY here, and family has to SHARE."

Larry: "No. No they don't. Some families murder each other. Don't you watch the news? No sharing. No SOAP."

3. EXT. STREET WITH SHOPS – DAY (ONE)
Larry is entering a convenience store. He sees a display of Cracker Jack at the front counter of the store, takes a box and purchases it.

[*SCENE TRANSITION*]

Larry is walking along the street eating handfuls of the Cracker Jack. While chewing, Larry pauses, chews a few times, pauses, then swallows. Larry pours some of the Cracker Jack into his hand and examines it (*there's only popcorn—no peanuts*).

Larry: "No nuts?"
Larry peers into the box and shakes it.

Larry: "NO NUTS!"

Larry peers into the box again and shakes it.

Larry: "And NO PRIZE! Unbelievable…"

Larry returns to the convenience store.

[SCENE TRANSITION]

Larry approaches the clerk and asks to return the Cracker Jack for a refund.

Larry (to the clerk): "It has no nuts and no prize. See, (*Larry holds up the box and points*) it says right on the box, 'candy-coated popcorn and peanuts'….where are the peanuts?"

(*Larry dumps the box on the counter as proof*). The clerk refuses to refund the purchase and points out the '800' telephone number on the package and tells Larry he has to call the manufacturer. Larry takes the box and leaves.

4. INT. LARRY'S OFFICE – DAY (ONE)
Larry is at his desk holding the box of Cracker Jack in one hand and the phone in the other. Larry is explaining that he bought the box and it contained no nuts and no prize

(*repeats several times*). The person on the other end (*unheard*) offers a replacement to Larry. Larry repeats the offer out loud.

Larry: "So you're going to send me a replacement box? Two boxes? Very good. And you guarantee they will have nuts and prizes? Yes, overnight delivery would be satisfactory. Send it to Larry David at 212 Vance Street, Pacific Palisades."

Larry hangs up the phone with a look of satisfaction.

5. INT. WOMAN'S APARTMENT – DAY-NIGHT (ONE)

Larry approaches an apartment to pick up his date. Larry knocks on the door. A woman answers and invites Larry in. Larry looks around the room and seems confused.

Larry: "Something's different…Did you get a new piece of furniture?"

Woman (rearranging knickknacks on a shelf): "No."

Larry (pointing to furniture): "Was that over here last week?"

Woman (making numerous/small changes to furniture placement-orientation): "Oh, that. That's what I was telling you about at dinner the other night. I practice Feng Shui."

Larry: "Is that like Kung Fu?"

Woman (continues making small changes to the furniture placement): "Stop it. You know I'm serious about this. It's a Chinese system that uses the laws of both Heaven and

Earth to help improve your life by receiving positive ch'i (chee)."

Larry: "You know, that reminds me, I could go for a nice Iced-CHEE....and maybe a side of CHEE-toes, or a ..."

Woman (still making small changes to furniture placement, interrupts Larry): "Stop RIGHT there. I take this very serious. I could NEVER be with a man ...you know, intimately...that didn't respect the power of Feng Shui...you even agreed to try it last week when I suggested we should Feng Shui you."

Larry: "Oh, is that what you meant?...Okay, let's gets the Feng out of here and go to dinner."

6. EXT. FARMERS MARKET – DAY (TWO)
Larry and Jeff exit Larry's car and walk into a farmer's street market. Larry and Jeff take numerous free samples and eat them. Larry tells Jeff about the date with the woman that is hung up on rearranging furniture.
Larry tells Jeff that she wants to rearrange his house so that he can have positive ch'i (CHEE).

Jeff (taking a bite of a sample): "Positive Cheese? That reminds me of shitty book that was made into a movie."

Larry: "ch'i (CHEE)....it's a Chinese thing....part of Fung GO...or Kung Pow...or something...I can't remember."

Larry and Jeff each pick out a carton of kiwi fruit to purchase and both get in line to pay. Larry notices a woman in front of him (in line) with extremely hairy arms. Larry turns and discreetly makes comments to Jeff and compares the woman's arm to his kiwi fruit. A woman standing behind Larry tells him she is the hairy-armed woman's daughter and rips Larry for being rude and making crude remarks. The daughter explains that it's medical related. Larry apologizes directly to the daughter (without speaking to the hairy-armed woman). Larry asks the daughter if the mother/hairy armed woman has thought to invest in laser hair removal or one of those lady-razors. Jeff makes several throat-cutting gestures at Larry. The daughter displays a look of shock/disgust and turns away. Larry turns to Jeff and shrugs.

7. INT. JEFF'S HOUSE - KITCHEN – DAY (TWO)
Jeff and Larry are in Jeff's kitchen. Jeff unpacks his farmer's market bag. Jeff criticizes Larry for making the hairy arm comments. Jeff hesitantly/reluctantly reveals to Larry that Susie has a similar condition having hairy arms.

Jeff: "It's a hormonal thing...but she gets them waxed."

Larry tells Jeff he will try and be more sensitive about it and not make any Chewbacca jokes when he sees her. Jeff reacts and tells Larry NEVER to say anything about it to Susie as she's overly sensitive about that subject. Jeff's phone rings. He examines the caller ID and tells Larry it's that pestering talent agent, Richard Dick.

Larry: "Richard Dick? Can't he afford a last name?"

Jeff: "Uhhhh, Larry, you have two...never mind."

Jeff answers the phone. The agent invites Jeff and Larry to a celebrity BBQ networking event. Jeff replies that he has to check his appointment book and rustles the farmers market bag pretending to turn pages. Jeff tells the agent he has a conflict and can't attend but volunteers Larry will go.

Larry: "I'll go WHERE for WHAT?"

Jeff (to the agent): "Yeah, Larry's right here and says he'd LOVE to be THERE for THAT. Yes, he'll be there."

Jeff ends the call.

Larry: "Was it because of the Chewbacca remark?"

8. INT. LARRY'S HOUSE – LIVING ROOM – DAY-NIGHT (TWO)

Larry and the Feng Shui woman are in Larry's living room. Larry is sitting on the sofa, pouring glasses of wine and trying to convince the woman to sit. The woman is moving Larry's furniture. She drags tables away from chairs and moves numerous objects to other parts of the room.

Woman: "There. Can you feel the energy?"

Larry (gesturing to the sofa): "I will…when you sit down over here."

The woman walks to the sofa and sits next to Larry. Larry takes the wine glasses off the coffee table and hands her one.

Woman: "No good."

Larry: "The wine? You haven't even tasted it."

Woman: "No, Larry. These tables (*pointing to the coffee table and end table*). They're blocking the positive energy."

Larry: "They are? Taste the wine. You'll feel the energy."

Woman: "No. They need to go over here." (*woman gives Larry her wine glass, drags the tables to the opposite side of the room, and returns to the sofa.*)

Larry (looking across the room at the tables): "What do we do with the wine? (*looking for a place to set the glasses*)"

The Feng Shui woman takes both glasses from Larry and swallows each glassful in one gulp.

Larry: "I LOVE IT."

Larry stands, pours the woman another tall glass of wine and dims the lights.

Larry: "I can feel the positive energy, can you?"

The woman takes the wine glass from Larry, take several long sips, and slides closer to Larry on the sofa.

9. INT. JEFF'S OFFICE – DAY (THREE)
Larry enters Jeff's office (*limping*) using a cane and wearing a small bandage on his forehead.

Jeff: "I guess I don't' have to ask how the date went with the cheese woman?"

Larry: "Ch'i, not cheese. I got Feng Shui-ed."

Jeff: "Congratulations. She must be a wildcat to have you using a cane."

Larry: "Not THAT. Feng Shui. She moved all my furniture around. I think she even got up after we had sex and rearranged the closets. I practically killed myself getting up in the middle of the night to take a leak. She moved furniture into the hallway. In the dark, I tripped on a floor lamp and nearly broke my neck. Who puts a floor lamp in the middle of a hallway?"

Jeff: "People pay good money for that."

Larry: "What? For sex? Or getting injured after sex?"

Jeff: "The Feng-Shui. People pay big bucks for someone to come in and do that shit."

Larry: "I don't think my health insurance will cover Feng-Shui. Where's the form you wanted me to sign? --- I gotta run. I'm meeting Richard for lunch over at that place on Lincoln."

Larry signs a document and leaves.

10. EXT. CITY STREET SCENE – DAY (THREE)
Larry and Richard Lewis are walking/talking on a busy city street (Lincoln Boulevard). Richards asks Larry about the cane and bandage. Larry tells Richard he got Feng-Shui-ed by his girlfriend. Richard is confused. Before Larry can answer, he steps in a wad of gum. Larry is irritated and ranting about it to Richard as he uses his cane to 'flick' the gum off the bottom of his shoe. The gum attaches to his cane and stretches (*like a rubber band*) from his shoe and

eventually 'snaps' off the shoe and cane. The gum wad flies through the air (*slow-motion shot*) into a convertible car (*top down*) that is passing by. The car zig-zags and keeps going.

11. INT. LARRY'S OFFICE – DAY (THREE)
Larry is on the phone at his desk discussing particulars of the celebrity BBQ with an unknown person. Wanda Sykes approaches the door, looks in, and hesitates. Larry waves her in. Larry continues to talk on the phone about the BBQ.

Larry: "No, no pork. Maybe burgers...veggie burgers? Sure....what? Ribs?....Hang on, there's someone here I can ask."

Larry asks Wanda a question about the cooking time for ribs and Wanda rips him for the racial association.

Larry (into the phone as Wanda berates him): "Let's stick with burgers. I'll get back to you."

Larry hangs up the phone.

12. INT. LARRY HOUSE – DAY (THREE)
Leon is sitting alone on the living room sofa inside Larry's house. Leon has a water glass in his hand and turns to put it on the end table (*that has been moved/is no longer in its original place*). As Leon is looking for a place to rest the glass, the doorbell rings. Leon gets up and answers the door. A delivery man tells Leon he has two boxes of Cracker Jack for Larry David. The deliveryman asks Leon, 'Where do you want them?' Leon doesn't know and calls Larry at his office. Larry answers and tells Leon he doesn't care.

Larry: "You called me about two lousy boxes of Cracker Jack?? Put them anywhere!"

The delivery man wheels in two oversized cartons of Cracker Jack (*boxes labeled: Cracker Jack – Quantity: 120*). Leon returns to the sofa and sits, holding a water glass (*tight camera shot of Leon*). (*Camera pulls back*), Leon is using one carton of Cracker Jack as a coffee table/foot rest (*with his feet up on the box*) and the other carton standing on its side next to the sofa as an end table. Leon places the water glass on the box and nods in approval.

13. EXT. CELEBRITY BARBEQUE IN SPRAWLING BACKYARD – DAY (FOUR)

Larry arrives at the celebrity BBQ. It is hosted in the backyard of a large house with 10 gas grills set up across an extensive, sprawling lawn. Larry is met by an event assistant who assures him all the details are taken care of. All Larry has to do is put the food on the grill and watch it cook. A camera crew will be going from grill to grill and may ask him to 'open the grill.' The assistant hands Larry a chef's hat, an apron with the words 'Celebrity Chef' across the front and tells him he's assigned to BBQ Grill #9. Larry goes to BBQ Grill #9 and finds the food for grilling is pork ribs.

Larry: "A Jew cooking pork? I DON'T think so."

Larry looks at the adjoining grills. Larry sees that Grill #8 is stocked with veggie burgers. Larry switches/moves his grill number '#9' to Grill #8 and puts the '#8' tag on the pork ribs grill. Standing at the next grill (#7), two people are chatting. One is wearing the 'chef' hat and 'celebrity' apron.

The other person is the hairy-armed woman from the farmers market (Scene 6). Larry recognizes her and approaches. Larry notices a 'bald' spot on her hairy arm and inquires about it. The hairy-armed woman tells Larry how rude people can be.

Hairy-armed woman: "Just the other day, some ASSHOLE threw gum at me while I was driving down Lincoln Boulevard. It got entangled in my arm and I had to have the gum cut out."
(*Larry 'replays' the gum-shoe incident and the slow-motion flick of gum, in his head – VIDEO REPLAY*).

Larry wishes her well and excuses himself. He returns to his grill and starts cooking the veggie burgers. Larry checks the grill. Larry turns the grill dial up to the HIGH setting, closes the grill cover for a few seconds and re-opens the cover to check. Slightly raising the grill cover, a blast of orange flames escape from the grill. Larry immediately closes the cover. Larry's cell phone rings. Larry turns to the hairy-armed woman and asks if she can watch the burgers on the grill 'just for a second' as he has to take the call and doesn't want to be 'RUDE' by taking a phone call around the other people. The hairy-armed woman agrees. Larry asks her to 'flip the burgers in a minute or so' and then walks away to nearby trees. (*A news/gossip TV camera-crew is seen in the background as Larry walks away*). Larry continues talking on the phone. In the background, an orange flame-flare up can be seen coming from his grill. Larry doesn't notice it.

Larry (into the phone): "Yeah, the BBQ is OK. I gotta run. I need to take a degner before I go back to my grill."

Larry walks toward the house removing his 'Celebrity Chef' apron. Larry enters the house. Sirens are heard (*audio dub*) in the background. The TV camera-crew is seen in the background heading towards Larry's grill. Larry emerges from the house adjusting his waistband and putting the 'Celebrity Chef' apron back on. Larry walks back to his grill. A crowd has gathered. The hairy-armed woman is on a stretcher with her arms bandaged. Larry looks worried, and pushes his way through crowd.

Larry: "WHAT happened to that woman?"

Bystander (to Larry): "The paramedics are taking her away...she's badly burned her arms."

Larry (yells): "Wait, WAIT!"
Larry moves to the side of the hairy-armed woman lying on the stretcher.

Larry: "Did you FLIP my burgers?" The TV camera crew focuses/closes up on Larry. Larry looks directly into the camera.

14. EXT. FARMERS MARKET – DAY (FIVE)
Larry and Jeff are at the farmers market, talking about the celebrity BBQ the previous day. They are at a food stand, receiving their food order (veggie burgers) and turn to walk away from the vendor stand. A man approaches them and introduces himself as a TV show producer. Jeff and Larry both recognize his name. He tells Larry he saw him at the celebrity BBQ the previous day. Larry's reaction is 'muted'. Larry starts to explain.

Larry: "I couldn't have foreseen the situation...that woman had no business getting so close to an open flame, and..."

The TV show producer interrupts Larry.

TV Producer: "Larry, you're a NATURAL. Listen, I have a food show I'm creating and you would be my ideal host." The TV producer gives Larry and Jeff his card, tells them to call him, and leaves. Larry and Jeff debate the proposal, 'is he legit?...what was the last thing he did? etc.'

Jeff: "Let's go over there (gesturing) when we finish these (burgers)...they have Cracker Jack!"

Larry takes a big bite of his veggie burger while looking at the business card. As he pulls the burger away from his mouth, a long dark strand of hair stretches from his mouth to the burger.

FADE OUT/Cue Music.

(END)

- 17 -
Ironies – Up Close *and* Personal

Doctor (to Ray): "You will feel some pressure...try not to fight it. Tell me more about this sitcom..."

Ray: "Yes, the sitcom...so Larry walks into the restaurant with a bandage on his arm while talking on his cellphone with Jeff and says out loud, 'I have a little prick that's bleeding all over the place!'."

There are moments when humor is appropriate. This wasn't one of them. Ray was chatting with his doctor during an annual checkup and mentioned he was writing sitcom scripts. The doctor took an immediate interest and asked him to describe some of the material. Ray launched into the opening scenes from "What a Prick" (an episode from Volume 2). Unfortunately, Ray's timing was...inappropriate. Ray hit some of the funniest spots just as the doctor was performing his final check—the prostate exam. The doctor, according to Ray, shook with laughter.

Ray: "UhhhHHHHHHHHH..."
Doctor: "THAT was funny..."
Ray: "Not for me"
Doctor: "Yes---very funny. We're all done here. Let me get you a paper towel to clean yourself."

The doctor gave Ray a paper towel and mentioned how much he enjoys the Curb Your Enthusiasm series because of his cousin, Jeff. Ray was distracted by the paper towel, but composed himself long enough ask: "Jeff? As in Garlin?" Yes. Ironically, Jeff Garlin is the doctor's cousin. Ray contemplated what to do next. The doctor seemed to enjoy our material, but, is it appropriate to ask a man who's just had his finger in your backside to give a set of

[150]

scripts from a couple of complete unknowns to an established actor-director-producer? Hang onto that thought for a moment.

Another irony-opportunity had presented itself. Jeff Garlin announced a series of stand-up shows he would perform in Chicago. We bought tickets, assembled our material and went to the theater. After the show, Jeff graciously greeted the attendees, and we cleverly staged ourselves at the end of the line. We approached with a two-sided plan. Ray had already met Jeff several times and Jeff recognized him. As Ray was complimenting Jeff on the performance and subtly shifting the conversation to future projects, John extracted a modified copy of the script for 'Good Things Come to Those Who Weigh(t)'. The modification was to the cover page. We changed it to read: 'Written by Jeff Garlin' in large block print. John offered it to Jeff with the line, "I found this on the floor—I think you must have dropped it." Jeff appeared puzzled, but accepted it. It only took him a moment to recognize what it was and he immediately dropped it as if it were a used piece of toilet paper, telling us, "Nooooo, I can't accept that. Larry prepares all his own material. I can't even look at it." Ray tried to keep the conversation going, but it was another dead end.

Back to the towel—the paper towel the doctor gave Ray. Ray: "Doc. This feels like a 220 grit…what am I supposed to do with this, refinish furniture?" The doctor apologized to Ray, telling him it was a recycled product and they were trying to go 'green' at the office. Ray couldn't contain himself: "Green? Doc…if I use this on my ass, it's gonna be RED…I'm better off using a page from one of my scripts." The doctor laughed and told Ray he should use that idea in his scripts.

The doctor was right…and Ray had another inspiration. With all the smooth dialog we've written, a page from our scripts would be velvety, silky, and *Scriptably*……

- 18 -

Episode 9

"Scriptably Soft"

Synopsis: Retracing his steps to find a misplaced TV script, Larry locates it in the hands of a Panhandler who extorts a large sum of money from Larry in exchange for returning it, only to discover pages are missing.

Scenes: 14

Cast: Larry, Jeff, Susie, HBO office staff, ALL-Clear/Colo-SHINE executive.

Special Guest(s): Gary Busey as the Panhandler.

"Scriptably Soft"

1. INT. GREENE'S HOUSE DINING ROOM - DAY–NIGHT (ONE)

Larry is at the Greene's house. Jeff and Larry are sitting at the dining room table as Susie brings out dinner. Jeff is warning Larry not to be surprised or shocked.

Jeff: "Susie has joined a startup company and she's been on this sort of health kick."

Susie brings out dinner on a tray. The tray holds three huge plates with tiny servings, including a serving of tablets.

Larry examines the tray.

Larry: "I'll skip the appetizers. What's the main course?"

Susie rips into Larry and tells him they all need to eat healthier. Susie tells Larry she's with a startup company that is the future of health maintenance: Colo-SHINE. As they begin to eat, Susie explains to Larry the concept of Colo-Hyrdo therapy. Susie shows Larry color pictures and drawings of intestines. She explains that food residues are lying in his colon and begin to ferment and putrefy. The rotting matter is passing into his bloodstream and is polluting his body at this very moment. Larry pushes his plate away.

Larry: "I'm full."

Jeff: "Yep, me too."

Jeff and Larry ask Susie for permission to be excused. Susie berates them for not eating healthy and tells them to leave the table. Jeff tells Larry they need to discuss some business and move to his (home) office. They stand and leave the table.

2. INT. GREENE'S HOUSE – OFFICE – DAY-NIGHT (ONE)

Larry and Jeff are entering his home office. Jeff looks back over his shoulder towards Susie as he's closing the door.

Jeff (excessively loud): "Larry, I got a call from that producer about a show…"

The door shuts. Larry looks at Jeff as he scrambles towards his desk.

Larry: "Whaddya got??"

Jeff opens a drawer, rapidly pulling items out and throwing them on the desk.

Jeff: "Crackers, pretzels, some cookies, a few gummies…"

Jeff and Larry wrestle over the packages, tear them open (spilling on the desk) and devour the contents, sharing with each other.

Susie (*off camera*): "Jeffrey?"

Jeff and Larry push all the junk food into a drawer and sweep away the crumbs on the desk. Jeff motions to Larry to brush the crumbs off his face as the door opens. Susie comes in carrying several small bottles of clear liquid, labeled 'ALL Clear HYDRO+'. She gives them to Larry and tells them they are body-hydrating formulas. She tells Larry if he drinks one per day, it will totally clear his body of pollutants within one week.

Susie: "And, it's Piña Colada flavored. Enjoy."

3. INT. LARRY'S OFFICE – DAY (TWO)
Larry is on the phone with Jeff. Jeff tells Larry he has sent a pilot script about a food show to Larry's office via messenger and is enthusiastic about it. Jeff insists Larry read it immediately. Jeff tells Larry it's not a regular script...it's a lot of 'free form'...there's A LOT of lines that say: 'LARRY-IMPROVISE something.' Larry is resistant.

Larry: "I don't think so. I don't like the concept of doing a show that's so unscripted." (*Larry looks directly into the camera for a moment.*)

Jeff tells Larry the script is from the TV producer that approached them at the farmers market (*at the end of 'HAIRS LOOKING AT YOU' episode*) after the celebrity BBQ. The producer wants Larry to host the food show. The script arrives while Larry is on the phone with Jeff.

Larry: "Yeah, it arrived. I promise, I'm reading it this very moment."

Larry immediately drops the script on his cluttered desk, mentions/reminds Jeff of their golf date later in the week and ends the call. Larry shuffles through the pile of papers on his desk, drinking coffee, dozing off. He repeatedly looks at the unopened script and pushes it further to the edge of the desk.

4. INT. HBO EXECUTIVE'S OFFICE – DAY (THREE)

Larry is sitting in an executive's office at HBO sipping from a cup of coffee. They are finishing a discussion about a historical movie project. Larry stands, thanks the HBO executive, says goodbye, and begins to leave the office. Larry is carrying the food show TV script with him and puts it under his arm as he leaves the office. Larry pauses at the door.

Larry (to the executive): "Let me ask you something...ever thought about producing a food or cooking show?"

The HBO executive is critical of the idea, says it's overdone, that every B-list wannabe has one, and unless the show has a truly unique angle, it wouldn't even show on local access. Larry nods and leaves. As Larry exits the office, he says *(to himself/out loud)*, 'I should use the restroom before leaving...and read this script.' Larry approaches the restroom *(in a hallway outside the HBO office door)* and tries to open the door. The door is labeled 'HBO Office restroom' and is locked. Larry 'listens' at the door, then knocks. While knocking, an office worker approaches to use bathroom. He has a key for the restroom and tells Larry the door requires a key that can only be obtained from the front desk. Larry waits/stands at the bathroom door as the man goes in. The man comes out of the bathroom, but won't let Larry in.

Office worker: "You have to get the key from the front desk."

Larry argues with him. The office worker blocks the door, refuses to give the key to Larry and leaves. Larry returns to the front desk *(holding the script)* and asks the receptionist for 'THE key'. (*The key is hanging from a hook by itself, clearly labeled 'Restroom'*).

Receptionist: "Which key?"

Larry: "Which key? The restroom...there's only one key there." (*gesturing to key hanging from hook.*)

Receptionist: "Why?"

Larry (irritated): "What do you mean, why? WHY? Because I have to take a degner."

Larry snatches the key from the receptionist's hand and walks to the restroom. Inside the stall (*sitting*), Larry pages through the script. Larry places the script on the tank lid behind him as he stands up. As Larry is 'finishing', he uses up the last of the toilet paper roll in the stall and cannot find a replacement roll. Larry retrieves a napkin out of his pocket and uses it to open the stall lock. Larry leaves the bathroom irritated/grumbling that the toilet paper ran out, and forgets/leaves the script on the tank. The restroom key is seen hanging out of his pocket.

5. EXT. STREET IN FRONT OF HBO OFFICES – DAY (THREE)
As Larry exits the office building, he finds/realizes he still has the key, but doesn't want to go back up to return it. Larry spots a well-dressed panhandler (Gary Busey) in front of the building and offers him $5 to take the key up to the 9th floor and return it to the front desk. The panhandler agrees. Larry pays him, gives him the key, and leaves.

6. EXT. GOLF COURSE – DAY (FOUR)

Larry and Jeff are at the golf course. Larry has just hit onto the fairway and Jeff is teeing up. Jeff asks Larry about the ALL Clear HYDRO+ as he hits (*onto the fairway, near Larry's ball*). Larry tells Jeff he hasn't tried it but brought two bottles with him. Larry tells Jeff he should try it.

Jeff (childlike): "I'm not gonna try it, you try it."

Larry suggests they try it together and hands Jeff a bottle. They open the bottles, toast/clink the bottles and Larry gestures as if to take a drink but fakes it to get Jeff to taste it first. Jeff drinks and shrugs. Larry takes a sip, shrugs, and comments, 'Not bad.' They walk onto the fairway chatting and sipping from the bottles. They hit from the fairway and continue to walk and sip. As they approach Jeff's ball, Larry and Jeff's stomachs rumble (*audio dub*). Larry and Jeff look at each other and simultaneously say, 'Colo-SHINE.'

[*SCENE TRANSITION*]

Larry and Jeff are shown running up the fairway, leaving their golf bags behind. Larry is clutching his stomach with one hand and carrying his golf club in the other. Larry throws his club aside, grabs his stomach with both hands and continues to run. Jeff is clutching his stomach with one hand and his butt with the other.

7. INT. JEFF'S HOUSE – DAY (FIVE)

Larry and Jeff are sitting in Jeff's home office. Jeff is wiping the sweat off his forehead with a cloth.

Jeff: "What are we gonna do?"

Larry: "I don't know. Should we tell her? We can't drink another drop of that stuff."

Jeff: "We can't tell her. She'll take it personally...and after yesterday, my ass is too sore to absorb the kind of ass-kicking she would give me."

Larry nods. Susie enters. Susie hands survey-comment cards to Larry and Jeff.

Susie: "I need to have you fill out these follow-up comment cards for the Colo-SHINE ALL Clear. Just check the boxes and put down anything you thought significant... you know, like the taste was good, or the texture was smooth."

Susie puts an envelope on the desk and tells them to put the cards in the envelope when they're done. Susie gives Larry two more bottles of ALL Clear HYDRO+ and leaves. Jeff and Larry discuss the comments (*out loud*) and write them in as they discuss.

Jeff: "It made me crap out a sandwich that I ate in the third grade."

Larry: "After drinking it, I passed a bobby pin from my mom's sewing kit that I swallowed when I was 9."

Jeff: "Suggest new marketing slogan – 'cleans like a white tornado'."

Larry: "Possible use as legal alternative to water-boarding."

Jeff: "Bottle should have a label on it that says 'do not drink and drive'."

Larry: "Should package with a disposable diaper."

Jeff: "Do the liquid drain opener ('Drain-O') people make this?"

Jeff takes both survey cards, places them in the envelope and tells Larry he will mail it in anonymously. Larry puts the two bottles of ALL Clear HYDRO + in his pocket and tells Jeff he can use them to clean the rust off his garden shovel.

8. INT. LARRY'S HOUSE – DAY (SIX)
Larry is sitting in his kitchen having coffee. Larry gets a phone call from Jeff.

Jeff: "How was the script – fabulous, right?"

Larry visualizes putting script on top of toilet tank (*REPLAY SCENE*) and realizes he left it there. Larry tells Jeff he's having a minor emergency and will call him back.

9. INT. COLO-SHINE EXEC OFFICES – DAY (SIX)
A Colo-SHINE marketing executive is sitting at his desk. He has the comment cards written by Larry and Jeff in front of him. A knock is heard on the executive's office door and Susie enters ('you wanted to see me?'). The executive asks if the comment cards are the actual survey-comment cards that she gave to her trial participant numbers 86 and 99? (*executive looks at the cards*). Susie replies 'yes', and she 'has many more like that.' Susie tells the executive she has been so busy getting the product out she's behind on the

cards, but 'the response so far has been very powerful.' The executive nods to Susie and repeats. 'Powerful, yes, they are certainly POWERFUL.' The executive reads some of the comments from Larry and Jeff's comment cards out loud (alternating).

Susie: "uhhhh, those quotes were taken out of context...and they were misquoted....one of them has Tourette's...I'm sure that it's..."

Colo-SHINE Executive (interrupts Susie): "Let me try another powerful phrase on YOU: You're FIRED."

Susie: "Wait until I get a hold of that fat fuck and his four-eyed puppet..."

10. INT. HBO EXECUTIVE OFFICE – DAY (SIX)
Larry races into the HBO office and asks the front receptionist for the restroom key. The receptionist remembers Larry and rips him for not returning the key the previous afternoon. She tells him it was their last key and now the room is locked while they wait for a locksmith to come out and change the lock. Larry defends himself stating that he sent the key back by special messenger and says he'll check with the messenger service.

11. EXT. STREET IN FRONT OF HBO OFFICES – DAY (SIX)
Larry exits the HBO office and looks up and down the street for the panhandler. Larry spots him, approaches, and asks why he didn't return the restroom key. The panhandler tells Larry he decided to keep it—he likes having access to a private restroom. Larry asks for the key and the panhandler declines.

Panhandler: "I'm sorry. You can't have it. I don't want the restroom to get dirty."

Larry offers to buy the key and the panhandler declines.

Panhandler: "Maybe I can rent you the key...but you'll have to pay the fee in advance and leave a security deposit for the key."

Larry relents, pays him and gets the key.

12. INT. HBO EXEC OFFICE – DAY (SIX)
Larry approaches the HBO office restroom door with the key in his hand. Larry uses the key, enters the restroom and goes to the stall but can't find the script. Larry checks/looks over the entire restroom, but the script is not there.

13. EXT. STREET IN FRONT OF HBO OFFICES – DAY (SIX)
Larry exits the HBO office building with the restroom key in his hand and goes to the panhandler to retrieve his security deposit. The panhandler questions Larry on cleaning up after himself and asks if he left some toilet paper. While trading remarks with the panhandler, Larry spots the script in the panhandler's shopping cart filled with his belongings. Larry demands the script back. The panhandler offers to sell it to him. Larry agrees and buys it. As Larry is flipping through the script, he notices pages are missing and asks the panhandler where the pages are?

Panhandler: "Someone used all the toilet paper in the restroom, so I had to IMPROVISE."

Larry turns to leave, pauses, reaches into his pocket and

pulls out two bottles of ALL Clear HYDRO+. Larry offers them to the panhandler as a tip.

Larry: "These are vitamin waters. They're flavored like Piña Colada...rum, pineapple and coconut...mix them together. You'll LOVE IT."

The panhandler takes them both. Larry smiles and leaves.

14. INT. HBO OFFICE – DAY (SEVEN)

In the hallway outside the HBO office, the panhandler approaches the restroom door holding a half-empty bottle of ALL Clear HYDRO+ in one hand and clutching his butt with the other. He drops the bottle, pulls the key from his pocket and tries furiously to open the door. The key does not fit and the door remains locked. The panhandler listens at the door, bangs on the door, waits, and then tries to force the handle. The door does not open.

FADE OUT.

A loud fart noise is heard (*audio dub*). The panhandler (*heard, not seen*) groans/curses.

Cue Music.

(END)

- 19 -

Mis-Perception and Miss Confection

Ray: I thought you were my friend?
John: Jesus Loves You...NOT me.

The above was an exchange we would utter in times of stress. It wasn't hurtful or said in anger, it was meant to break the tension. After six months of commuting to Los Angeles from Chicago every week, we uttered it a lot.

There's a certain amount of sacrifice and certain degree of opportunity that comes with living a Monday through Friday life in one city, and spending Saturday-Sunday in another. Ray's divorce wasn't complete and John hadn't found the courage to unwind the relationship with his girlfriend in Chicago. At the time, it was important to both of us that we didn't cross the line between honesty and dishonesty. Understand that we both grew up near Chicago, where they say things like "It's not REALLY dishonest until you're indicted AND convicted." Not for us.

Life in Los Angeles was turning into something other than a walk on the beach. It occurred to us that we were being cheated out of our lives by having to commute to LA every week. We were being cheated financially by working nightshift and still having to participate in dayshift company activities. And, it turned out, one of our significant others had been cheating (seeing someone else) while we were in LA.

Then, from the unlikeliest of places, once again we found motivation, inspiration, and vision. The World's WORST Boss came through for us with this golden e-mail:

"We will be having some serious discussions as to your dedication to this project, and on what you are spending your time while you are deployed. There are many perceptions as to what is going on out there and the amount of time you are actually spending working, and it would behoove you to change those perceptions."

Behoove? Who 'talks' like that? At the same time, we were receiving letters of commendation from the Los Angeles location's top manager, and notes of gratitude from the various departments we dealt with.

Shortly thereafter, Ray's divorce was complete, John was free of his girlfriend, and opportunity was knocking. It was time to answer. We shortened our long night-shifts and would not participate in day shift work activities. We stopped responding to the pointless text messages and threatening e-mail from the World's WORST Boss, and we resumed *living*. Ray has a tremendous gift when it comes to talking to people – especially women. It took all of a week for him to meet and start dating an executive chef in LA. John would also start up a relationship with a woman in LA. The tension went away and life became a great big chocolate soufflé.

One of our favorite escapes was a sidewalk café in El Segundo, California. It was an excellent source for a 'wake-up' coffee after 8pm (since we started our workday around 11pm) and we wrote countless sitcom scenes sitting there. This place made a terrific cappuccino and was staffed by a stunning and exceptionally sweet hostess and occasionally, a knockout waitress. Ray wanted one...or perhaps both. Ray was working his magic on the hostess for a week or so when we noticed that every time she came over to our table to chat, the 'cook' came out of the back and glared at us. He was big, angry-looking and paced back and forth in a menacing way. We laughingly referred to him as 'KILLER'. Ray was working his way up to asking the hostess on a date when she finally admitted 'KILLER' was her husband. OOPS. Time to find a new coffee spot.

One of our other stops for coffee was a small bakery near our hotel. Ray struck up a conversation with the cute pastry-dessert baker and was dating her within a week. This had mixed results, but served a purpose. Ray determined that dating two women concurrently was a matter of logistics. "If I time it right, it's like a perfectly constructed tiramisu."

But logistics can work for you or against you. One evening, Ray was in a hurry to finish one dinner date with the pastry baker in order to start a second dinner date with the executive chef. Ray promised to bring dessert for the dinner date with the chef, but didn't have time to buy anything. Ray used the excuse of needing to go to work to leave the first dinner, but not before asking his date (the pastry baker) to wrap up the amazing dessert she had prepared for them for him to take away. She did, and Ray took the dessert to his second dinner date that evening (with the executive chef). What Ray overlooked was the private note the baker had slipped into the dessert package.

Dating more than one woman at a time has inherent risks.

Having them find out about each other can be troubling.

Having them meet is surely a recipe for *HOT, Crossed...*

Episode 10

"HOT, Crossed, Buns"

Synopsis: Larry has double the trouble when dating a baker and a chef at the same time. Larry's problems multiply when he reluctantly agrees to host a TV-cooking show that seems doomed from the start and ends with a Jerry Springer style twist.

Scenes: 12

Cast: Larry, Jeff, Leon, Larry's Admin/Antoinette, Richard Lewis, Larry's girlfriend #1 (Cook), Larry's girlfriend #2 (Baker), TV Show Producer, TV Show Director, Adult Phone Service Agent (voice over), Cooking Show audience.

Special Guests: Two well-known adult film stars (such as Jesse Jane or Riley Steele and Misty Stone or Marie Luv).

"HOT, Crossed, Buns"

1. OPENING SCENE – INT. LARRY'S OFFICE – DAY (ONE)

Larry's cell phone is ringing. Larry answers and it's an adult phone-sex service agent that wants to 'talk dirty' to Larry. Larry is confused.

Larry: "Let me ask you something? Don't people usually CALL the service, not the other way around?"

Agent (*audio dub*): "It's a new marketing initiative—like a community reach-out program. A lot of people may not be aware of our service and we want to spread the word."

Larry is confused and resists. He tells the agent he's not interested. The adult service agent pleads with him and starts talking 'dirty'. Larry plays along for a few seconds.

Larry: "You want to do WHAT to me? With coconut oil? I can't, I have high cholesterol. What? Why? Is that even possible? A twin sister? I have a weak back."

Larry's admin assistant walks into his office.

Larry (to the agent): "I'm sorry, the whipped cream sounds nice, but I'm lactose intolerant. Good bye."

Larry's admin wants to know what the call was about. Larry explains that it was a phone-sex service, but THEY called him.

The phone rings again, Larry looks at the phone, reaches for it and hesitates. He picks it up and it's Jeff.

Jeff (*audio dub*): "Hey, it's me. I just wanted to remind you that you're hosting the taping of the cooking show tomorrow. Don't to be late, don't worry, and have fun. You'll LOVE it."

Larry is less than enthusiastic.

Jeff (*audio dub*): "And wait until you meet the co-host, you'll LOVE her, too."

Larry is caught off-guard and objects.

Larry: "CO-HOST? WHAT CO-HOST?"

Jeff (*audio dub*): "Don't sweat it. She's a Julia Child type – someone that will do ALL the work. You do the intro, make some funny, witty remarks during the show, then sample some food. It's that easy."

Larry is still resistant and makes a remark about some old Betty Crocker bag from the 1950's and this just isn't for him. Jeff reminds him it pays $100,000 per episode. Larry ends the call.

2. INT. LUNCH AT RESTAURANT– DAY (ONE)
Larry is seated at a table with Richard Lewis, finishing lunch. Larry is telling Richard about the two women he's dating concurrently. One is a gourmet chef and the other is a specialty (dessert) baker. Larry tells Richard he's going on a double date that night. Richard questions the 'double date' reference and tells Larry it doesn't mean what he thinks it means. Larry explains that he's going to the chef's house for dinner and then going to the baker's apartment for dessert. Richard expresses his concern. Larry's cell

phone rings. Larry tells Richard it's the chef calling. Larry answers. The chef asks Larry if he would bring a dessert for their date night. Larry agrees and ends call. Larry asks Richard to wait a moment, and calls the baker. Larry asks to re-arrange their date to an early-evening get-together because he has a business commitment later in the evening. The baker agrees and Larry ends the call. Richard is dumbfounded by Larry's calls. Larry explains to Richard that he moved the baker date first so that he can get dessert from her to take to the chef's house for the dinner date. Richard tells Larry that sooner or later, one or both will find out he's double dating and will poison his food. Larry dismisses Richard's remark and asks for the check.

3. INT. GIRLFRIEND-BAKER'S APARTMENT - DAY-NIGHT (ONE)

Larry is at the door of the apartment of the baker – girlfriend. The baker opens the door wearing an apron covered in flour and greets Larry. She tells Larry he's early. Larry apologizes and pushes into the apartment. Larry rushes the evening - gulping his coffee and taking only sample-size bites of the desserts. Larry tells the baker-girlfriend he is hosting a cooking show and will be taping over the next two days. The baker-girlfriend tells Larry she would love to go and see him. Larry tells her he will get her a ticket when he goes to the studio the next day. Larry tells the baker-girlfriend he's pressed for time and must leave for his business commitment. He asks her for the dessert 'to-go'. The baker-girlfriend wraps dessert into a foil shaped swan and hands it to Larry. Larry apologizes for rushing out and leaves.

4. INT. GIRLFRIEND-CHEF'S HOUSE - DAY-NIGHT (ONE)

Larry is at the door of the house of the chef–girlfriend. The chef opens the door wearing an apron splattered with sauce/gravy and greets Larry. She tells Larry he's late. Larry apologizes and pushes into the house holding the dessert. The foil swan's neck is bent and the head is turned sideways. The chef stares at it and frowns at Larry. Larry asks how soon until dinner?
[*SCENE TRANSITION*]

Larry and the chef are sitting at the dining room table as the chef unwraps the dessert. She samples it and tells Larry it's fantastic. She wants to know where Larry got it and what's in it. Larry tells her it was from his personal baker and it's an old secret family recipe. Larry tells the chef-girlfriend he is hosting a cooking show and will be taping over the next two days. The chef-girlfriend tells Larry she would love to go and see him. Larry tells her he will get her a ticket when he goes to the studio the next day. Larry tells the chef the dinner was fantastic, but he must leave to prepare for his show the next day. Larry apologizes for rushing out and leaves.

5. INT. FILM STUDIO/STAGE OF THE COOKING SHOW – DAY (TWO)

Larry is on the set. The show producer is with Larry and introduces him to the cooking show director. The director is sitting at a table, poorly dressed, eating lunch (*dropping food on his clothes*) and asks Larry to sit. The director spits a wad of gum onto the table. While eating lunch, the director spits seed/nut shells from his food onto the floor. The director takes a drink from a glass of wine and 'backwashes' food bits into the glass (visibly floating in the wine). The director insists Larry try some: 'taste this wine' and pushes the glass with the floating food bits into Larry's hand. Larry makes excuses.

Larry: "I can't, thanks, I'm a borderline alcoholic, (*pause*), it runs in the family, (*pause*), it claimed the life of my mother before I was born."

Larry puts the glass back on the table. The producer turns to the director and tells him he has to step away for a minute.

Producer: "Excuse me, I have to take a degner. I'll be back in five."

The producer starts to leave. Larry stops him and asks him what he just said? The producer is surprised by Larry's question.

Producer: "What do you mean? EVERYONE knows what 'taking a degner' means."

Larry (animated/excited): "Of course I know what it means. I invented the phrase."

The producer rolls his eyes and mocks Larry.

Producer: "Sure, Billy. Sure you did."

Larry: "That's, LARRY"

Producer: "Whatever."

[*SCENE TRANSITION*]

ON THE SET OF THE COOKING SHOW

The cooking show intros are heard (*audio dub*) as Larry stands off camera waiting to enter the set. Just before Larry walks onto the set, the director tells him the original co-host was replaced at the last minute. The original co-host was hospitalized. Larry asks why. The director is evasive in replying.

Director: "Some sort of stomach thing, I think."

Larry: "Food poisoning?"

Director: "No, she was caught with some sort of inside trading scheme by the SEC and it caused her some...digestive stress disorder or something..."

Larry is 'announced' (*audio dub*) on the set and walks on camera (*visibly disturbed*). Larry's co-host (off screen) is introduced, 'One of Americas leading adult entertainment stars' and she walks on camera. Jesse Jane/Riley Steel (blonde bombshell adult film actress) walks up beside Larry and greets him with a hug and kiss on the lips. (*Larry looks her up and down.*) Larry reverses his mood and is visibly enthusiastic (*audience laughs loudly*). Larry trades banter with the co-host and makes some subtle porn jokes/references. The co-host is quick witted and teases Larry. She tells the audience she can cook onscreen and off. Larry asks what's on the menu and co-host starlet replies, in porn lingo, 'whatever you can afford.' Larry picks up a card, purposely reads slowly and announces the dishes incorrectly. The audience laughs, applauds, and cheers (*audio dub*).

The cooking show proceeds and Larry makes comments as the co-host starlet prepares the dish. The starlet repeatedly does sexy things - holds a sausage up to her mouth, slowly licks her fingers, bends over to get things out of the oven (*showing her ass*), and makes 'sexy references' to the recipe-dish (rump roast). Larry starts to get 'turned on' by the starlet. Larry stares at her chest and begins to sweat and stumble over his words. Larry takes a slice of white bread and starts soaking up the sweat on his head. Larry checks the progress of the dish and opens the oven. A small fire can be seen inside. Larry immediately closes the oven and moves away.

Larry (to starlet): "Do you have excess hair on your arms?"

Starlet: "Sweety, you won't find a hair ANYWHERE below my neck."
(*Audio dub: audience cheers wildly*)

The starlet pulls out the 'finished' (previously prepared), dish from under the counter, asks Larry if he wants 'a TASTE', and seductively feeds Larry. Before Larry can recover, the co-host announces because this is the inaugural show, she invited her own special guest to help with dessert: 'Hot Chocolate'. The starlet asks for a big HOT welcome for her friend (black porn star, Misty Stone or Marie Luv). The guest star prepares hot chocolate (*using the whipped-cream, seductively*). The guest star offers Larry 'a TASTE' (*licking her lips*). The guest star kisses Larry and gives the co-host a long kiss on the lips as the show ends. The audience (*camera pans the crowd*) is cheering wildly and applauding (*audio dub*). Larry leaves the set and quickly walks to the exit.

7. EXT. LARRY (IN HIS CAR) DRIVING HOME – DAY (TWO)

Larry calls Jeff from his car. Jeff does not answer and Larry leaves a voice message.

Larry: "That was the WORST thing I've ever done. I can't go back tomorrow...I'm never doing it again. It was terrible...humiliating...embarrassing! If this ever gets broadcast, I'll have to move to Nepal...or someplace where TV doesn't exist!"

Larry instructs Jeff to call the director and let him know how terrible it was.

8. EXT. LARRY AT HOME – DAY (TWO)

Larry is at home telling Leon about the show and how dreadful it was. Leon wants to know if Larry 'tapped' the co-host or the guest star. Leon asks Larry to introduce him to the co-host and her friend. Leon asks if Larry can get a spot for him on the show, 'as a sous-chef or a sauceier.' Larry stares and says 'a saucey what?' Larry tells him to forget it...it will be cancelled before the first episode ever airs. Larry's phone rings. Jeff is calling. Larry answers.

Jeff: "You DID IT, Larry. You're IN. The preliminary reviews are in. It tested very well with the survey group. They really liked you and the co-hosts."

Jeff tells Larry that he explained Larry's concerns to the director and the director has agreed to the changes. 'You will now have more 'director input' to the show and will be responsible for key decisions.' Larry asks Jeff 'what kind of key decisions?' Jeff tells Larry he can choose the menu for each show. Larry is enthusiastic and says he likes the changes. Jeff tells Larry he will also have to provide the recipes for the menu he selects. Larry is less enthusiastic and says he doesn't like the changes. Jeff convinces Larry to give it one more try and reminds Larry that it earns him 100k per episode. Larry agrees and tells Jeff he can probably obtain recipes from his girlfriends, the chef and the baker, since he has a double date with them that night. Larry gets a call-waiting alert, tells Jeff it's his baker-girlfriend and he has to take the call. Larry takes the call from the baker-girlfriend and confirms their date at her apartment. She offers to make Larry a special dessert and asks Larry to bring something for dinner. Larry agrees and ends the call. Larry calls the chef-girlfriend and tells her he has a VIP pass for the cooking show and would like to drop it off for her…and maybe she could whip up something for dinner. The chef-girlfriend agrees and Larry ends the call. Larry's phone immediately rings. Larry answers and it's an adult phone-sex service agent and she wants to 'talk dirty' to Larry. Larry is (still) confused.

Larry: "Have we spoken before. Don't people usually call the service, not the other way around?"

The agent tells Larry it's their new marketing initiative and she has to make at least four complimentary calls per day. Larry tells the agent he's not interested. The adult agent ignores Larry's statement and starts talking 'dirty'. Larry sighs, covers the phone.

Larry: "Leon, it's for YOU."

9. INT. GIRLFRIEND-CHEF'S HOUSE - DAY-NIGHT (TWO)
Larry approaches the door of the house of the chef–

girlfriend. The chef-girlfriend opens the door wearing a white apron suggestively dotted with red sauce and greets Larry. She tells Larry he's early. Larry apologizes and pushes into the house. Larry rushes the evening but compliments the chef-girlfriend on dinner. Larry tells her the food was exquisite and asks for the recipe. The chef-girlfriend tells Larry it's an old secret family recipe and she can't give it out. Larry tells the chef-girlfriend the cooking show he hosted was a total disaster but he has to return and tape the second segment the next day. The chef-girlfriend tells Larry she would still like to go see the show. Larry pulls two VIP passes from his pocket, gives her one, and shoves the other back in his coat pocket. The chef-girlfriend tells Larry she wants to change into something comfortable (*winks*) and leaves the room. Larry walks to the kitchen counter and spots a rolodex card file open to the dinner recipe card. Larry tries to gently remove the card and ends up ripping it out of the file. The chef-girlfriend returns wearing a negligee. Larry tells her he has to prepare for the show taping and must leave. Larry asks if she could make him a plate 'to-go'. The chef-girlfriend wraps dinner into foil shaped like a penis and gives it to Larry. Larry doesn't notice the shape and leaves.

10. INT. GIRLFRIEND-BAKER'S APARTMENT - DAY- NIGHT (TWO)

Larry approaches the door of the apartment of the baker-girlfriend. The baker-girlfriend opens the door wearing an apron and nothing else and greets Larry. She tells Larry he's late. Larry apologizes and pushes into the apartment. Larry presents the dinner and realizes the foil is an obscene shape. The baker-girlfriend looks at the foil shape and comments to Larry, 'Nice, Larry. Subtle.' Larry rushes the evening, hurrying through dinner, coffee, and dessert.

Larry compliments the baker-girlfriend on the dessert. Larry tells her the taste was exquisite and asks for the recipe. The baker-girlfriend tells Larry it's an old secret family recipe and she can't give it out. Larry tells the baker-girlfriend the cooking show he hosted was a total disaster but he has to return and tape the second segment the next day. The baker-girlfriend tells Larry she would still like to see the show. Larry tells her he doesn't have any more VIP passes and will see if he can get her one at the next taping. The baker-girlfriend tells Larry she wants to change into something more comfortable (*winks*) and leaves the room. Larry walks to the kitchen counter and spots a Rolodex card file open to the dessert recipe. Larry tries to gently remove the card and ends up ripping it out of the Rolodex. Larry hears the baker-girlfriend returning and shoves the recipe card into his coat pocket. As he repeatedly pushes the recipe card into his coat pocket, he inadvertently/unknowingly pulls the out VIP pass to the cooking show and it falls to the floor. The baker-girlfriend re-appears wearing a negligee. Larry tells her he has to prepare for the show taping and must leave. Larry apologizes for rushing out and leaves.

11. INT. ON THE SET OF THE COOKING SHOW – DAY (THREE)

The cooking show intro's are heard (*audio dub*) as Larry stands off camera waiting to enter the set. Larry is introduced and walks on camera. Larry's co-host (off screen) is introduced and she walks on camera. Larry is visibly cautious and the co-host is dressed and acting suggestively (*audience cheers loudly as* the *camera-shot pans across the audience*). The chef-girlfriend and the baker-girlfriend are seated next to each other in the front row of the audience. Larry sees them. They both wave at him and notice each other waving at Larry. Larry (*nervous/distressed*) turns away from them and trades banter with his co-host. The co-host asks what's on the menu. Larry (*nervously*) pulls out the two recipe cards he stole the previous evening and reads them out loud. Larry reads the main dish: 'Smoked Meat in extra virgin olive oil.' The co-host makes remarks and gestures about being extra virgin and eating smoked meat. The chef-girlfriend recognizes the main dish recipe, becomes visibly irritated and starts to grumble. The chef-girlfriend 'mouths' to/at Larry, 'You Son of a Bitch.' Larry reads the dessert recipe, 'Hot Crossed Buns.' The baker-girlfriend recognizes the recipe, becomes visibly irritated and 'mouths' to/at Larry, 'You Son of a Bitch.' The baker-girlfriend starts to grumble ('that SOB stole my family-secret-recipe'). The chef-girlfriend turns to the baker-girlfriend and asks her to repeat that. The baker-girlfriend tells the chef-girlfriend that Larry stole the recipe from her during their date last night. The chef-girlfriend tells the baker-girlfriend that's a lie because Larry was with her last night and he stole HER recipe for the main dish. The two women argue louder and louder, yelling at each other and then at Larry for stealing their family-secret-recipes. The fight turns physical (*similar to a Jerry Springer episode*) and the women have to be restrained (*pulling hair, tearing clothes/bra's exposed/etc.*). The audience laughs, applauds, and cheers wildly (*audio dub*). The co-host turns away from the camera, looks over her shoulder into the camera and says, 'Todays feature, HOT, CROSSED, BUNS', and spanks her ass. Larry clutches his forehead. (*Audio dub: audience cheering wildly*).

12. EXT. LARRY (IN CAR) DRIVING HOME – DAY (THREE)
Larry's cell phone rings. It's Jeff calling. Larry answers.

Jeff: "Hey, it's me. The reviews are in. The show tested OFF THE CHARTS with the survey group. They LOVED it. The studio loved it. They loved you, Larry. How did you stage that fight? It was surreal...almost like Springer. They bought the full season...TEN EPISODES. And there's already sponsorship deals lining up...you'll make a FORTUNE."

Larry is speechless and hangs up. Larry's cell phone rings. Larry answers. It's the adult phone-sex service agent that previously called and wants to talk 'dirty' to Larry (*audio dub*). Larry sighs and agrees.

FADE OUT/Cue Music.

(END)

- 21 -
BUT WAIT! THERE'S MORE! VOLUME 2

In the end….there was light. We wrote this book. If you're reading this, someone paid for it…which means at least one copy sold, and that makes it A GREAT SUCCESS. We still have a few moves left. We continue to talk about stripping off all the 'Curb' references, renaming the characters, and shopping it around as a generic sitcom. Occasionally, we still tempt ourselves with the idea of self-producing a few parody episodes, using Curb actor look-alikes. Of course, the ones that are spot on doubles for characters can't act at all. The ones that can act have no resemblance to any Curb character and are better suited for a Baywatch-like sequel.

As the chapter title promises, *THERE'S* more. Volume 2 is already written and being finalized for printing. 10 more sensational episodes filled with special guests, fresh ideas, and the continuation of a theme or two that we developed in Volume 1. And yes, we have enough material for a Volume 3. But we're thinking of waiting for lawsuits to surface (or not) before we spend time on that. And speaking of lawsuits….

Personal Note to Larry David:
As much as we were inspired by all your various work (outside of Curb Your Enthusiasm), we discovered the huge fan base dedicated to Curb who are anticipating (demanding, really) future seasons. As we began putting our material and ideas together, our plan was simply to pass along a stack of scripts or outlines to you in hopes of inspiring a future episode or two. Once assembled, we realized we had over thirty episodes (and nearly degnered ourselves). We decided to compile them as individual seasons. Feel free to consider any of our material. Have your people contact our people…actually, we don't have any people…just email us at: **BigCarlProductions@gmail.com**

FADE OUT/Cue Music.

Ray & John

Printed in Great Britain
by Amazon.co.uk, Ltd.,
Marston Gate.